THE DIY SPRINKLER BOOK

Install Your Own Automatic Sprinkler System.
Save Thousands and Get the Satisfaction of Knowing
You Did It Yourself and did it RIGHT!!

By

Jonathan Lee

DISCLAIMER

When embarking upon any project or endeavor that requires physical exertion, it is always a good idea to make certain that you are physically up to the task at hand. Consult your physician if you are unsure as to whether or not this is the case. The content presented in this EBook is intended to be used for informational purposes and is not an endorsement of any particular reader's ability to undertake the actions or activities described herein. We take no responsibility or liability for injury, loss or damage incurred as the result of this information.

TABLE OF CONTENTS

WHY I WROTE THIS BOOK

I've always been drawn to "projects" – working on an old car, fixing things (or at least, trying to fix things) around the house, finishing furniture, etc. Like most people who undertake these sort of things, I've never really had any interest in doing any of it as a vocation. To me, the pressures that come from getting it done "on time and under budget" would likely ruin that pristine swell of satisfaction one gets from completing something TANGIBLE, something you can look at and enjoy every day as a testament to your work and planning.

The perspective of someone not deeply immersed in a given trade as a VOCATION is certainly different than someone who is. I purposely broke this project down to its elements, avoided the use of any terminology that would not be self-evident, and in short, attempted to make no assumptions that any part of this process was a 'given'.

There are many that can literally see a project – from start to finish –take place in their head. They know instantly what materials are needed, what needs to be done first, how much can be done per session, etc.

All good qualities to have, but luckily not really essential for the project that you are about to undertake – the one that prompted you to pick up this very e-book.

I, on the other hand, have always found it necessary to put pen to paper, while carefully and deliberately analyzing the task before me. Sure, there are times when I wish my skills were more innate, but on the other hand, this deliberate approach allows me to better appreciate the DETAILS of a project like this – the installation of an irrigation system – where the challenges may lie, why it is important to resist that temptation to cut corners, etc. and hopefully, better communicate them to you, the reader.

I'm convinced that the drive to "fix" things (or at least improve them) is innate in many of us – even those that don't have that natural ability I mentioned above. Maybe it's a drive to leave things better than we found them. Maybe it's a quest for that sense of accomplishment that can only come from seeing something through from start to finish.

On the other hand, maybe it is a drive to save money.

. . . .. Certainly nothing wrong with that.

Years back, I watched a movie called "The Edge", where Anthony Hopkins declares "What one man can do, another can do". I definitely believe this to be true– and also believe this ability is by no means limited to men.

Sure, we all have different aptitudes and abilities, and it's certainly not fair to compare oneself to someone who performs a given skill as a livelihood, but with enough practice, enough persistence and enough knowledge, there are a lot of skills that are learnable, a lot of accomplishments that are attainable.

This is one of them. And I KNOW that you can do this. How? Because I did. You can learn from my mistakes and not (hopefully) repeat them. The first irrigation project I undertook was tougher than the second, and so on.

Like many projects, one of the key elements is to accurately ASSESS what needs to be done and break it down into manageable (and understandable) steps. This is where this E-book comes in. Far from a pile of technical jargon, the information you are viewing on this very screen will take you through the steps necessary to get from start to finish. It's important to not skip steps, to not move forward until you understand what you are doing, to PAY ATTENTION to what you are doing and to have a clear outcome in mind – not only the finished outcome, but what you want to accomplish at each step along the way.

But do that, and I am confident you will get the finished result you are after.

It's all a matter of taking what may seem at first a fairly daunting task, and breaking it down into manageable pieces. And doing things this way, you will also give yourself the opportunity to UNDERSTAND those pieces, their proper sequence and how they fit together – from the preparation of the land you are working with, through to the choosing and installation of your landscaping.

All explained right here on these pages.

INTRODUCTION: The Process Explained

As was noted above, projects are almost always easier when you break them down into manageable steps. First, this makes the entire project seem a lot less intimidating. Secondly, this approach provides a sort of 'checklist' along the way to make sure nothing is left out.

In the case of THIS project, the steps to be accomplished are as follows:

ANALYZING WHAT YOU ARE STARTING WITH

This includes assessing the presence of weeds, semi-dormant grass, soil condition, any additional work that may be needed to grade or level the land you are working with, etc.

ANALYZING YOUR OWN CAPABILITIES AND COMFORT LEVEL

I did note at the outset that this is a project that most people can accomplish, but let's face it, our physical capabilities, time constraints, comfort level with physical labor and the use of tools/power tools all do vary. There are a few ways to approach this. You can go the solo route (as I have), enlist help with some of the manual labor, enlist help with manual labor and select steps along the way (I will say emphatically that you should hire a plumber to attach a tie in to your home's existing water system and an electrician or licensed handyman to create an access point for your system's electrical needs).

Or as an alternative, you can hire out ALL the labor for this project. Certainly no shame in that. Should you decide to go that route, I trust that you will still find the contents of this E-book helpful in creating a sort of blueprint as to how things should go if you delegate the project to others.

DETERMINING WHAT MATERIALS AND SUPPLIES YOU WILL NEED FOR THIS PROJECT

We will go over the tools and equipment that will be needed to get this project done. For purposes of organization, the actual materials needed (parts, supplies) will come separately. Some of these tools are ESSENTIAL, while others are suggested because they will make the job a lot easier. Some tools will be purchased. Others, you can make an individual decision as to what to buy and what to rent.

SOIL PREPARATION AND THE REMOVAL OF ANY EXISTING GRASS/WEEDS

Almost always, the land you are going to be working with will have some grass, weeds or a combination sitting on top of it. You will need to systematically remove this to start with a 'clean slate' as you begin the project. This may include simply killing the grass/weed combination if it is limited in quantity, or going a step further and cutting it out entirely if there is a lot more growth already in place.

There are likely some good reasons why the land you are starting with looks as it does, and perhaps chief among them is the fact that it takes PROPERLY PREPARED soil to support a healthy lawn. We'll go over the steps needed to transform the land as it exists now into a more fertile environment on which your lawn and plants to thrive.

PLANNING YOUR SYSTEM, INCLUDING CREATING YOUR SHOPPING LIST OF MATERIALS AND SUPPLIES

This is a fun part of the process. You'll want to spend some time to figure out just what you want your finished yard to look like – where you want a lawn, how many individual stations you will need, where you want flowerbeds, vegetable gardens or both. This may seem like a daunting task, but like most of the other steps, once broken down into smaller steps. In addition, there are some very valuable and cost effective (in some cases, FREE) resources that you can take advantage of to make this part a lot easier.

Done correctly, you can walk into your local home improvement store (well, likely a SUPERSTORE like Home Depot or Lowe's) armed with a shopping list. Further ahead, there's also a list of tools you will need to either rent or buy.

DIGGING TRENCHES AND BUILDING YOUR SYSTEM, BACKFILLING YOUR TRENCHES

This may also seem a little intimidating, but again, the key is to break things into manageable steps. Once you have properly designed your system, you'll know exactly where to place these trenches, what their width and depth should be, and how to properly connect one trench to another (where applicable) to avoid extra work. As well, there are ways to further automate this process, if you are so inclined.

Once your trenches are good to go, the building starts. A fun and rewarding part of the process, this is where you can really see your progress take hold. You will be starting with the MANIFOLD (in essence, the heart of your irrigation system) and extending all your plumbing out to where it needs to go to properly irrigate your lawn, flowerbed(s), vegetable garden, or a combination of these.

A professional-looking job depends heavily on details and finish work. Once your system is in place and tested, you will backfill the trenches, and take extra precautions to make sure the ground on which your finished landscaping will reside is nice and flat, free from any unwanted high spots, low spots or indentations.

INSTALLING AND WIRING YOUR TIMER

Perhaps the best thing about this project is the convenience it will provide in maintaining healthy landscaping. Once installed, an automated timer will allow you to preprogram when watering takes place and how long each portion of your property receives water. *(Because this portion of the process does put you in close proximity to your home's electrical system, it is very important that you or whomever you hire for this portion of the process, knows exactly where your home's wiring runs, so that it is not interfered with in any way.)*

ADDING YOUR LAWN, PLANTS, VEGETABLES/FRUIT, ETC.

With the system in place and a nicely prepared starting point, here is where you will need to make the decision as to whether you will be installing sod or seed (the pros and cons of each are discussed in detail) as well as what plant varieties, vegetables, fruits, etc. will be added. This is where your vision really becomes a reality. The individual irrigation needs of each of these will also be delved into.

So, let's get started.

ANALYZING WHAT YOU ARE STARTING WITH:

The first step in this, or nearly any project, is to assess the job in front of you. More often than not, when you step out to your front or back yard and have a look, you will see that you are starting with a plot of land that is covered with weeds, dead grass and compacted dirt. Likely very compacted dirt. It's certainly not an unusual situation - go take a walk up and down nearly any block, and the lawns that are not thriving nor maintained are usually like this, or fast heading towards it.

A neglected lawn didn't get that way overnight. First there were likely some dry or dead spots that showed up in an otherwise healthy lawn. Then weeds slowly began covering the lawn. Then more weeds. Perhaps the property owner relied on the self-discipline it takes to remember to haul out the manual lawn sprinkler, attach it to the garden hose, then systematically move it around from place to place on the lawn, or an inexpensive lawn service that came at increasingly rare intervals to 'mow and blow' the lawn and little else.

Too much trouble. Not enough time.

Once the lawn really showed its disrepair, it became an even bigger chore to look after. After all, what 's the point in weeding and watering a lawn that is not going to look good even after all that work?

Lawns with this kind of "back story" all tend to look the same. They don't exactly exude curb appeal, do they?

So, there are a variety of factors that need to be assessed as you embark on your project. What follows is a brief outline of these factors. Rest assured that each of these will be covered in more detail as the book later.

Weeds

What is now your lawn, or perhaps more accurately, the parched, compacted and neglected plot of land you seek to transform, is almost certain to be festooned with weeds. They are everywhere. Literally. Even relatively healthy lawns almost always have some weeds present.

It won't be worth your time to go out and buy the sort of "selective" product that kills the weed and spares the grass. This is for a couple of reasons.

First, at this stage it is pretty unlikely that you have an appreciable amount of viable lawn present. There are many varieties of weeds that look like grass. Allow enough of them to sprout up and thrive and you have what may appear to be a lawn, but is actually just a collection of healthy weeds. In most cases, there is little point in attempting such a surgical approach.

Second, while some of these products, such as those made by Bayer or Ortho, are actually pretty good at killing what are known as "broadleaf" weeds, they seem to be far less effective on more grass-like varieties. Generally speaking, the closer a weed looks to grass, the harder it is going to be to kill with a common herbicide that is designed to spare your lawn. It's been my experience that even those products claiming to kill grass-like weed varieties fail to do so with much consistency.

So, getting rid of weeds as you begin your project calls for a more decisive approach. You will want to go and select a product that kills both grass and weeds alike. There are quite a number of products on the shelf of your local nursery or home improvement shop, but the one you hear most about is Roundup. And not just because of the commercials. The stuff really does work. It is inexpensive, easy to use, and safe (when you follow the directions properly).

You would think that a product that performs a task such as this would also have a sort of half-life that would be so long as to make planting a lawn after its use something that could only be taken FAR into the future. Surprisingly, this is not true. Most products, Roundup included, will do their work so effectively, efficiently and quickly that, even with fairly heavy use, the affected area will be ready for planting around 72 hours later. But, as you'll see a little later, I don't recommend you do so quite so quickly.

Soil condition

My very first lawn project was quite a challenge, largely because of the condition of the soil. In much of Los Angeles, the soil tends to be mostly clay (which actually seems a little strange considering you always hear that Los Angeles is essentially a desert). So much so, that when I dug my first trench and set some of the soil off to the side on an unusually hot day, the sun actually dried the clay so that it became almost ceramic in consistency.

Clay soil is problematic for a number of reasons. For starters, as noted before, its tendency to dry to an almost rock-like consistency fairly easily, even between scheduled watering, makes the absorption of nutrients and water nearly impossible, and often is the cause for a lawn to begin a slow, steady decline, even with enough water. The clay acts as a barrier - keeping out all the things that a lawn needs to be healthy. The water may run over its surface, but gets no deeper, instead just sheeting off onto the sidewalk and street.

The solution? Well, there are products out there that CLAIM to turn clay soil into rich loam, capable of supporting nearly any plant life. Some even claim that all you have to do is merely spray them onto your lawn, and the rest takes care of itself. Seems too good to be true. In most cases, it is. In reality, when you are starting from scratch, as I assume you are, it's best to take the necessary steps to at least start with optimum soil conditions and that will require the addition of certain materials – gypsum and soil conditioner (readily available and not particularly expensive, either).

While you are probably familiar with soil conditioner, you may not be familiar with gypsum - a mineral compound composed of calcium, sulfur, and oxygen, mixed with water molecules. This compound results in a grainy, whitish product that will remedy clay soil, but only if used correctly. There is a particular way to apply it if you want good results.

Now, in some rare instances, soil condition, rather than being the consistency of clay, instead is too sandy, the functional opposite. These cases are generally a lot easier to deal with and require simply "cleaning" the sandy soil of any materials that do not belong there, then introducing nutrients that will enrich the soil to the extent it supports a healthy lawn or vegetation of your choosing.

How Level is Your Lot?

While a lawn can certainly grow even if not perfectly level you will want to have a pretty good idea what your finished work should look like, as far as the angle from house to street, side to side, etc. This will help a lot in figuring out just how much dirt you need to move around to get where you need to go, how you design your sprinkler system, etc.

Whatever plan you end up with, you DON'T want to end up with your house (whether it's on a foundation or a slab) at the lowest point of the lot. This will cause water to collect around the foundation, and if it reaches high enough, can cause serious damage to plaster, wood and nearly everything else it comes in contact with.

Your house doesn't necessarily need to be elevated relative to your yard, but it is a good idea to try and keep the ground around the foundation fairly level, then either continue that level line out toward the end of the property, or perhaps even figure in a slight downward angle. This will help insure that water does not pool next to your house.

It's also important is to make sure your lawn is fairly level from side to side, and has no low spots. While the former is really more for aesthetics, the latter will also help guarantee that, when you irrigate the lawn, each part gets approximately the same amount of water. During much of the year, this may not be all that important, but in the hotter months, it can make quite a difference, especially if you live in an area like Southern California, where water rationing may only permit you to run your sprinkler system twice per week (so you have to make the most of it). Eliminating the low spots can go a long way toward this.

ANALYZING YOUR OWN CAPABILITIES AND COMFORT LEVEL

While designing and installing your own sprinkler system is not rocket science, it does require physical labor. I have no way of knowing your individual situation, what your physical condition is, your affinity for physical exertion, your comfort or familiarity with power tools (or at least your willingness to learn their proper and safe operation, which is not particularly difficult), so I also have no way of knowing which parts of this project will seem clear as day and easy to accomplish, and which seem too much to take on.

This doesn't have to be gut-busting and all that arduous, and there are steps you can take to make things easier on yourself. For example, the more you automate things with the right equipment, the easier it gets. Regardless, this project may not be for everyone. There will be some digging, pushing and pulling equipment, etc., no matter how well you plan things. As I noted at the outset, you can also elect to outsource some or all of these steps to outside labor.

If, for example, you have known physical limitations – bad knees, a bad back, heart issues, etc. I would certainly recommend taking this into consideration. Nothing written on these pages should be taken as any kind of suggestion to exert yourself in a dangerous manner or above and beyond your physical limitations.

It is up to you to evaluate your own physical condition and decide if you are up to doing this yourself, in part by yourself, or farming the whole project out. Should you elect for the last approach, I am confident that this E-book will provide a trusty blueprint to keep you on top of the work that needs to be performed, and HOW this work needs to be performed.

And should you elect to go the solo route I am a big believer in parceling this project out in manageable pieces. It will save you unwarranted overexertion and makes the more manageable. As well, it will make it much easier to track your progress along the way.

WHEN TO GET HELP

For some, certain restrictions may come down to time – there just may not be enough hours in the day to put into this without giving something else short shrift, or extending the project for so long that it becomes unappealing. If this is the case, and even if you decide to enlist the services of others to do much of the work for you, again I am confident that this E-book will prove to be a valuable resource to help you assess the quality and accuracy of the work being done.

For still others, it may come down to expertise. Maybe you lack confidence in your ability to operate some of the machinery required. Maybe you don't like the idea of working with electricity. (Most people don't, actually). But luckily, unless you decide you want your system operating off of a stand-alone power supply (as opposed to simply plugging into a wall socket), there is actually very little to have to worry about in this regard.

So, what to do and what to farm out? Well, I will say this - Unless you have good confidence in your ability to tap into your existing water source (near the hose bib, most likely), I would definitely recommend having a LICENSED plumber to do this for you.

AND if you don't heed much of anything else in this E-book, do remember the following – ALWAYS CONSULT YOUR LOCAL POWER COMPANY BEFORE DOING ANY DIGGING WHATSOEVER. There should be no charge for sending a representative out to your residence to show exactly where your gas and water lines are, as well as any electrical lines (should your utilities be below-grade).

The consequences for not doing this can be disastrous, even deadly. It takes almost no force to rupture a natural gas line when you have a pick-axe in your hand. And you definitely do NOT want that to happen. So, be safe. Call your utility company out to show you where these potentially problematic areas are so that you can avoid them.

Again, there is certainly nothing wrong with farming out some or all of this work. Just as a point of reference, each time I have installed a system, I have enlisted the services of a plumber to make the tie in to the water source and if I were to opt for a stand-alone power supply for the sprinkler timer, (as opposed to simply plugging it into a socket) I would definitely hire an electrician to tie into a house electrical system. Why? Because my level of certainty in my ability to work with plumbing fittings or electricity is not sufficient to offset the relatively modest sum it would require to have someone come in and do the job correctly. Some readers are likely more intrepid than myself, some less so.

So, when confronted with this dilemma, just ask yourself "How confident am I in undertaking (insert part of the process here)? This should determine your actions.

A FEW TIPS ON ERGONOMICS

As you proceed on this project, one thing to try and keep in mind is that you should always try to do ALL work in the most comfortable position possible.

There are going to be tasks that can only be accomplished in what would be less than a full recline, but as you set about the various steps, try and take a few seconds to see how your positioning feels. Do your knees hurt? Is your back under strain? Are you breathing properly?

All are important things to consider. If you put in a few days' work and come away miserable, this whole process will start to seem a LOT harder than putting in the same amount of working and coming away from it with just a healthy sense of fatigue, and a good sense of accomplishment.

If the task at hand requires you to bend over for a long period of time, be conscious of your breathing. Any activity that causes you to double over makes breathing harder, your blood pressure higher, and fatigue to set in much faster.

Wherever possible, bring yourself down to the level of your work, or at least as close to it as possible. Sure, you may come away with stained clothing, but the discomfort you save yourself will be well worth it.

If you are digging out a ditch, for example, don't stand at the original ground level. Instead, get down to the level you have dug to, and work from there. Much less bending over, and therefore, much less work. Take this one step further and make sure the tools you are using have handles sufficiently long enough for you to go about your work in a comfortable position.

If you are operating a piece of machinery, let the machinery do the work. There is a tendency for many of us, myself included, to try and 'muscle' tools like rototillers or sod cutters, instead of just using your bodyweight to guide them as they do the task they were designed for. Just this tip alone will make a long day of work easier on your body.

I've found it is not a bad idea to try and 'warm up' a bit before undertaking anything strenuous. Take a few minutes and move around, stretch and get the blood flowing. Just as with any vigorous activity, you will also likely find that this will lessen muscle soreness at the end of the day.

When working outside for any length of time, it is also VERY important to keep yourself hydrated and protected with sunscreen. If you are anything like me, you get caught up in what you are doing, and before you know it, literally hours have elapsed. If you are out in the sun, or if it is a particularly hot and humid day, that means a lot of perspiring. And a lot of perspiring means you are becoming increasingly more dehydrated. Not good.

Try and make sure plenty of water is never far away. That way, you don't have to worry about resisting the temptation to "keep going" at the risk of your comfort, and in extreme cases, even your health.

Again, ALWAYS apply sun block when you are outside. Even when the sun doesn't seem all that intense.

SAFE TOOL USE

For the most part, installing an automatic sprinkler system revolves around the use of tools that are pretty common – shovels, picks, PVC cutters, etc. But if you do come across a tool that you are not totally familiar with, take a little time to make sure you are using that tool correctly. And again, LET THE TOOL DO THE WORK.

For power tools, safe operation is doubly important, as injury, perhaps even severe injury, can result from taking chances. I'm not looking to scare anyone away here. It's just worth noting that it's important to know how to use any given power tool before turning it on. Rest assured that as you start using these tools, you will become more proficient and confident in their use. Bottom line . . . before even flipping the switch, pulling the ripcord, etc. make sure you know how that tool operates and how to do operate it safely.

You can always ask about safe tool use from wherever you rent from. In the case of nearly all of the projects I have completed, I have rented most of my equipment from Home Depot (www.homedepot.com) or Hertz Equipment Rental (www.hertzequip.com). For the most part, I have found the employees of both companies to have helpful, knowledgeable staff that are pretty willing to show you how to safely operate whatever tool they put in your care.

CONSERVING ENERGY

When I got started with my first lawn project, I found myself making a LOT of unnecessary trips, back and forth, from the work site to where I kept my tools. These short trips don't seem like much of an energy drain, but over the course of an afternoon they are. Plus, they tend to take the focus off what you are working on, making you less efficient as your return to pick up where you left off.

So, you can conserve a LOT of energy just by properly planning out what you intend to work on, making a checklist of tools needed to get that task or tasks accomplished, and making sure you round up EVERYTHING that will be needed and keeping it within easy reach. Find a place where you won't be doing much reaching or bending to retrieve your supplies and tools, as these are big time energy sappers.

And, it really is worth repeating . . . **HYDRATION IS IMPORTANT**. Even being slightly dehydrated can mimic the feeling and symptoms of very low grade Chronic Fatigue Syndrome. And you can become dehydrated fairly quickly on a warm day if you are caught up in your work.

Make sure plenty of water is always close by.

Also, as you make your way through this E-book, I'd recommend you periodically ask yourself "Am I understanding this?" "Is this clear to me?" before proceeding. I'm pretty sure that, especially with a second glance, everything contained in these pages will be easy enough to grasp, but I wouldn't recommend getting so overanxious as to plow forward before understanding the individual steps required to get the job done. Rest assured that here are many (myself included) who first approached this with no experience, and got just the result they wanted.

"What one man can do, another can do."

Remember?"

DETERMINING WHAT MATERIALS AND SUPPLIES YOU'LL NEED FOR THIS PROJECT

To an extent, each lawn project is a little bit distinct in what equipment, planning and preparation it requires. Certainly, the smaller the plot of land to work with, the easier the task, and the shorter time to completion. Regardless, there is equipment that you will need to complete this project. All of it is readily available (either by renting, or owning) at your local home improvement center.

A BRIEF RUNDOWN OF THE TOOLS YOU'LL NEED TO GET STARTED:

Garden rake, shovel, hose and measuring tape

A Common Garden Hose (essential) – Low tech? Sure, but you will be surprised how much easier it is to use a hose that is sturdy and leak-free than merely grabbing the cheapest one you can find. You may have one sitting coiled outside your house right now, and it may well be good enough to do the trick. But if it already has leaks, crimps too easily, etc., you may want to think about replacing it to save yourself some time and aggravation, as those leaks only get worse over time.

A good quality garden hose will prove plenty useful – for a variety of functions – wetting dirt to make it easier to work with or to get it to settle, using water pressure to tunnel under a sidewalk in certain situations (armed with an attachment you can either buy or make yourself) and of course, cleaning yourself off before going inside after a day's work. Available at any hardware or home improvement store.

Shovel (essential) It may seem that a shovel is a shovel, but there are actually a number of different types out there. Some are specifically designed to dig trenches. Narrower than its traditional counterpart, a trenching shovel will prove useful if, after designing your system (more on that later) you find that you are only running one or two PVC line per trench. More on this later.

In areas where you will be running multiple PVC lines (and illustrations to follow will show how you can do this properly) you will probably find that a wider shovel will be more useful. In most cases, there are going to be areas where multiple lines are running side by side, then branch off on their own. Available at any hardware or home improvement store.

Measuring Tape (essential) - You probably have one lying around already and you'll get plenty of use out of it as you are planning things out. Don't rely on eyeballing distances from sprinkler to sprinkler, etc. Uniformity and accuracy are what you will be striving for, and this humble tool will help you get there.

Rake (essential) – A nice, sturdy metal rake, (as opposed to the plastic kind you would use for raking leaves, etc.) is very handy for redistributing dirt or topsoil, leveling out low or high spots, and separating weeds, dead grass or anything else for easy disposal. A landscaping rake will feature an extra wide profile that will allow you to work a wider path with each pass, and is all the more useful for this project, though not essential.

To the left is the Yard Boss, by Stihl. This is considered more of an automated tilling tool for flowerbeds and small plots of land but can be used for larger projects, provided you're up to making more passes, due to the noticeably narrower footprint and less power. On the other hand, once purchased it never has to be returned, and is on hand for future gardening projects.

Rototiller (optional but definitely a time and energy saver) - Unless you are working with a very small plot of land, you are likely to get a lot of use out of this piece of equipment, as it's definitely a chore to till soil by hand. It's possible but a chore. A rototiller loosens dirt by means of motor-powered set of teeth that dig in, rotate, and "spit out" the dirt. Alternatively, it is certainly possible to till a yard by hand, using a pick, but it's a lot of work and is therefore not for everyone. For a beginner, the use of any motorized equipment may seem a little intimidating at first, but this particular piece of equipment is very easy and safe to use, as long as certain precautions are adhered to.

In my own case, I found this piece of equipment to be so indispensable that I opted to BUY and not rent, a rototiller. The particular one I chose, the Stihl Yard Boss, is actually smaller than the type you would normally rent, but surprisingly durable and up to the task.

While most people will opt to rent this piece of equipment. In my case, I just rationalized that even though the initial cost was considerably higher than renting a rototiller from a home improvement store, and (because of its smaller size), the model I chose actually requires more passes to accomplish the same results, I would not have to return it on a deadline, and I knew it would come in handy for other projects in the future.

I was actually right about this.

And, it's actually proven to be a pretty sturdy piece of equipment. I've used the Yard Boss to till an entire 40' x 30' front lawn (a not inconsiderable plot of land), with no problem at all. And again, while the narrower width of the blades means more trips back and forth, I have found that the lighter weight and easier maneuverability cancel much of this effort out. Lastly, because I own it and don't have to return to the home improvement store to rent it repeatedly, the Yard Boss is on hand in my tool shed whenever I need it to loosen up flower beds, etc.

So, in my case, this put the decision to buy and not rent over the top for me. Your situation may be different, but if you plan on doing much serious gardening in the future, it is not a bad piece of equipment to have.

I have no vested interest in Stihl as a brand. I've just found the general consensus to be that they are sturdier than many of their counterparts. You may opt for another brand, or simply rent, and there is certainly nothing wrong with either of those choices.

Available at most improvement stores (or in the case of the Stihl Yard Boss) at select retailers.

Sod Cutter (recommended, depending on yard size) - More often than not, you will be starting to work on a plot of land that has some sort of existing lawn, even if it's made up of just weeds and dead grass. With enough planning and effort, you could get rid of it by hand, using a pick, shovel and other tools. I've done this myself, but if you are working with a yard of any size, you may want to consider renting a sod cutter.

The sod cutter is another motorized piece of equipment, also fairly easy to use. It features a blade that cuts downward, then rotates side to side, so that it cuts and lifts off a predetermined amount of grass/dirt from your yard. This will result in pieces of discarded strips that will roll up like a carpet for disposal. It's definitely easier to work with and much faster than having to swing a pick into the soil to accomplish the same thing.

Trencher (optional) - You can dig your trenches by hand using a shovel, but this piece of equipment, though a bit more unwieldy than a rototiller, does save time and effort. I would consider this piece of equipment somewhat less essential than a rototiller, as it seems more often than not, trenches for this project are dug by hand, using a shovel. Available at most home improvement stores with rental departments.

Commonly found in the plumbing section of most home improvement stores, convenience packs like this will include most of the tools needed to install and repair irrigation fittings, including a PVC cutter, small blade screwdriver, Teflon tape and an extractor for removing broken pieces of PVC risers.

PVC Cutter (essential) – This plier-like tool makes short work of cutting the PVC pipe that comprises the backbone of an irrigation system. Effective for any PVC pipe that is 1 ½" or less (though there are some that handle larger diameters than that), the use of this tool is WAY easier than doggedly cutting lengths of PVC pipe with a hacksaw, and a lot more precise. Often, this tool comes in a 'convenience package' where it is teamed up with a couple of other 'sprinkler-related' specialized tools.

PVC Extractor, Small Blade screwdrivers (essential)- I've lumped these in together, as they often come prepackaged, as shown in the example photo above. The extractor will allow you to more easily remove sprinkler risers that may have been cut improperly, or further down the line, perhaps damaged by a lawnmower (it will eventually happen). It's WAY more convenient than trying to grab hold of a relatively small piece of PVC tubing with a pair of pliers. The small blade screwdrivers (both standard and Phillips head) will be needed further down the line to adjust the throw of your sprinkler heads, tighten down fittings, etc.

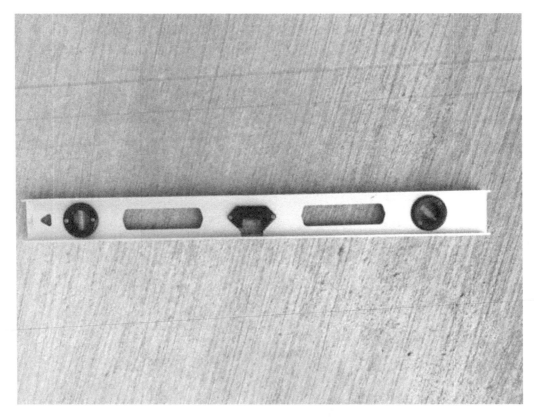

A carpenter's level. This will prove useful to obtain a professional looking result as you assemble your system.

Level (not strictly essential, but certainly recommended) - Remember the paragraph above, where I noted that the mark of a professional looking job lies in the details? Well, having a carpenter's level handy will certainly make a difference in the overall look and professionalism of this project. Its proper use will help guarantee that your sprinklers are situated properly and that your other fittings are not needlessly tilted to one side – which would make them less efficient in some cases and simply look goofy and amateurish in others. To save a few bucks, you can also go to a more specialized place, like Harbor Freight here in California, to purchase a SMALL level, as you are not likely going to be needing anything very large for this purpose.

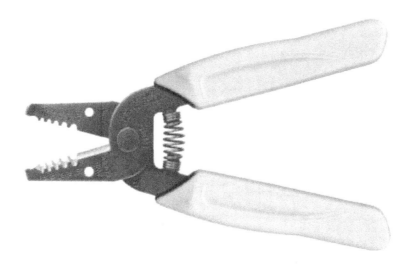

Wire cutter/Wire Stripper (fairly essential) – When it comes time to connect wiring from your timer to your manifold, this tool will definitely come in handy. Also somewhat plier-like, it features a straight edge that can be used to cut the length of a prepackaged wire or set of wires, and also features a series of grooves that allow wiring to be easily and accurately stripped of its coating (without cutting the wires themselves) so that connections to timer and manifold valves can be made.

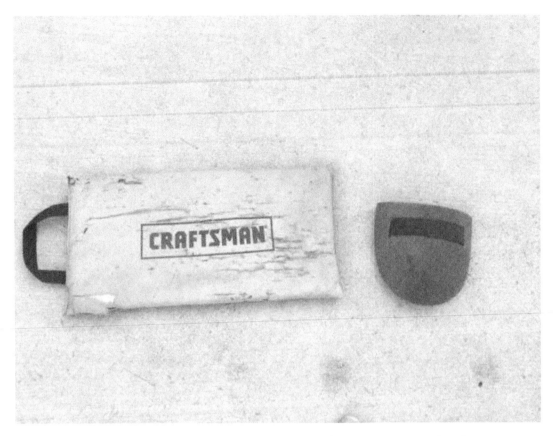

Well-worn from lots of use, a cushion designed for protection as you kneel, alongside the more common kneepad.

***Knee Pads/Knee Cushion (not essential . . . but)* -** You will be doing a lot of kneeling during this project. You can get by without these, but not sure why you would choose to do so. At the low end, a pair of neoprene knee pads with Velcro straps will take some of the stress off your knees as they make contact with the group. To a point, the more you are willing to spend, the greater the degree of comfort with these, but even the entry level models make a difference, especially over the course of a day or days.

An alternative I also like, and in some ways find preferable to knee pads, is a knee cushion, like the one shown below. Firmly padded, yet very lightweight, it is easily moved from place to place and really does provide comfort.

Gloves (ABSOLUTELY ESSENTIAL) By all means, go out and get yourself a good pair of gloves. Probably several would be a good idea. Even the toughest of hands will blister after the repeated use of a shovel, hoe or other piece of garden equipment. And when this happens, you are going to be less inclined to get back to it quickly. That I can speak on first hand.

Support or Lifting Belt (varies by individual) While I don't use one myself, I can see the benefit for some of wearing a SUPPORT belt or device. Unlike a gym belt, these are nylon devices that fit around the torso, BUT ARE NOT MADE TO WEAR TIGHT. This is an important point. Often times I see constructions workers and others involved in manual labor, wearing weightlifting belts and cinching them up pretty tight even when they are not engaged in heavy lifting, or other higher activities that exert stress on one's core.

This is a mixed bag – and the negatives (to me, anyway) outweigh the positives. If you are lifting objects you are concerned may strain your back, then by all means, go out and get a support belt. But, just know that there can be a downside as well. These belts may well be worn for a considerable amount of time in one session. Cinched too tightly, they DEFINITELY hinder your proper breathing and can even give you a bit of a chafe. Just some factors to consider.

A manure spreader. This is used, not surprisingly, to spread manure or any other type of seed cover or fertilizer, evenly across the yard. Usually, they have a detachable handle that makes them a bit easier to transport in a car, but take care to protect your upholstery should that prove to be your means of transportation. That grate-like surface on the cylinder can damage your car pretty easily.

Manure spreader (essential only if you opt to use seed, and not sod) This cylindrically shaped rolling tool has large perforations in its rolling 'drum' through which seed cover passes, so that it is evenly distributed in a uniform layer. If you opt for sod, then this tool would not be used.

Seed Spreader (essential if you opt to use seed and not sod). This is another rolling, 'walk behind' tool. A seed spreader features a fairly large capacity bin, at the bottom of which is a spinning arm that 'spreads' grass seed in an even pattern and is powered by the motion of its wheels moving forward as you push it. This tool is also not needed if you opt to use sod.

5-gallon plastic bucket (essential, but could be something you can borrow)
Water Pressure gauge with a hose bib adapter (essential)

SUPPLIES YOU'LL NEED

Unlike the tools listed above, these are not broken down into essential vs. non-essential, as you will be NEEDING these items to get the job done. None are particularly expensive. You will, however, need to plan your trips to your home improvement center in advance, because for example, PVC pipe comes in 8' lengths (minimum) and while it can certainly be cut down to smaller lengths to fit inside your car, you may instead want to track down a more appropriate vehicle so that you won't have to join so many small pieces back together as you create your system. ***PLEASE NOTE THAT, FOR THE PURPOSES OF THIS EBOOK, WE WILL BE USING ¾" DIAMETER PVC PIPE AND ¾" FITTINGS.*** You could conceivably go with 1" as well, but ¾" should work fine for most applications and is most common.

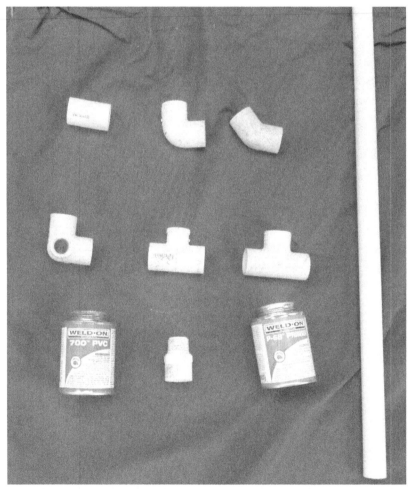

PVC fittings in a variety of shapes and uses, along with a length of standard Schedule 40 PVC tubing, PVC primer and PVC glue

PVC Pipe PVC pipe will make up the 'skeleton' of your entire irrigation system. Lightweight, waterproof, and very durable, you will find PVC very easy to work with and prepare, even if you have never done so before. At many stores, you will see more than one type of PVC pipe, so always opt for the "Schedule 40" designation as it features thicker walls and is therefore sturdier than the only slightly cheaper Schedule 120 and is well worth the extra few pennies (literally) per piece.

PVC Fittings – Available in quite a variety of angles, functions and diameters, these fittings are what connect pipe to pipe, pipe to valve, and what also allow you to navigate corners, PVC intersections, etc.

A quick walk down this aisle of your home improvement store (these parts are usually located in the "plumbing" section) will reveal just how many specialized parts there are for this purpose. If you were to go to a store that specializes in landscape equipment, you would likely see even more.

While I think you will find it is easier to conceptualize the use of these fittings by planning in order of their use (from your water source, out to the sprinkler heads themselves), following are the most commonly used pieces:

WHY ALL THESE SHAPES AND SIZES? THEY ALL SERVE A SPECIFIC PURPOSE.

Couplings These tube shaped parts are sized so that a PVC pipe fits snugly inside each half of them, with the two entering pipes separated by a small raised portion in the very center of the coupling. You will end up using a LOT of these, as they are needed anytime you are joining two lengths of PVC pipe. That is going to happen a LOT. Always make sure that the couplings you buy are the right size to accommodate the pipe your using with them. Most often, you will be using parts based on ¾" diameter PVC. There can be some exceptions – as going to a 1" diameter pipe will generally increase the available water flow. By far, ¾" piping and PVC parts are most common.

Elbows These are available most commonly in a 90 degree turn, which allows you to position one pipe perpendicular to another as you are turning corners, etc. A well-stocked home improvement store or landscape supply store will also have these in a 120 degree turn, which is perfect for less dramatic turns, or for working around immoveable obstacles in your yard.

T's There's a right way and a wrong way to route the plumbing for your system, and T's will allow you do things the right way. Instead of sending water from your water source to the sprinklers in continuous, circuitous and winding path, you will want to divert your water supply in several directions (more on this a little later). This is what T's do.

Threaded male/female adapter Sounds like a complicated part, but it isn't. The threaded portion of this part attaches to the bottom of the valve itself. The other, "slip" end of the part is where the plumbing for your system will extend downward from both the front and back parts of the valve as the PVC extends outward from the valves to the respectively sprinklers. Not clear yet? I think it will be easiest to follow the use of this part as we start the actual installation process.

T with threaded ½" opening for riser - The opening at the bottom of a sprinkler body is designed to accommodate a ½" threaded riser (shown a bit further ahead). So, it is important to make sure that the part you are using to attach the riser to the pipes is sized to accommodate this.

The T shown above is what you will need. Fitted with ¾" openings to accommodate PVC at both ends, the third hole in the T is sized and threaded to accommodate the black, threaded PVC riser that, in turn, fits in the bottom of the sprinkler body.

ELBOW WITH ½" threaded opening - This part performs the same function as the T, but is used to position sprinklers/sprinkler risers at the end of a pipe, as opposed to "in line" along a section of pipe, or at a junction of two pipes.

There are a number of other specially designed PVC parts as well, but the ones described and pictured above are what will be most commonly used. You may want to familiarize yourself with some of these other parts, just in case you find that they would make your project that much easier.

PVC Cement – This is literally the glue that holds it all together. PVC cement is brushed onto any two PVC pieces that will be joined together. It dries VERY quickly, which can be both good and bad. Good, in that it will allow you to work faster and get more done, bad in that, if you make a mistake, you have either very little or no time to correct it before the glue sets. So, when gluing parts, it makes a lot of sense to DOUBLE CHECK what you are doing before embarking on this step.

PVC Primer – Purple in color (usually), this substance is what you will brush on the surface of any two (or more) pieces of PVC you will be connecting together. It helps provide a slip free, clean surface for PVC cement to adhere to, helping to guarantee strong, leak- free connections. Just know that this primer will stain pretty much anything it comes in contact with, be it clothes, surrounding items, or even the PVC pipes themselves.

And, as far as this staining is concerned - while, in my opinion there is really no way to make PVC piping look attractive, no doubt the PVC parts that will be visible (the manifold, where your valves attach) DO look better free of stains. So you have a couple of choices as to how to proceed on this . . .Be REALLY careful to avoid staining, resign yourself to some stains (less important if this area is really out of sight), paint the visible parts (Krylon is one brand that now makes paint that will adhere to PVC) or most commonly, go out and get a purpose made plastic covering designed to fit over and cover your valves.

Teflon tape being wrapped around a sprinkler riser to create a water tight seal. You'll want to do this wherever there will be a substantial amount of pressure on the fitting.

Teflon Tape (essential) – While all of the actual SUPPLIES should be seen as essential, I want to emphasize that it is important NOT to skip using Teflon tape on the proper connections.

A WORD OF CAUTION WHEN SHOPPING

When you start buying your PVC parts at your local home improvement store, just bear in mind that NO parts are more commonly strewn about their area than are PVC fittings. Most commonly displayed in boxes that are cut in half to display their contents, shoppers routinely pick these parts up, inspect them, and put them back in the wrong display box before moving on. Always make sure that the part you are grabbing out of the box matches the description ON the box, and that it is what you are looking for.

WHAT TO RENT, WHAT TO OWN

Luckily, installing a system is not all that tool dependent. There are tools that will make the installation of the system, and its subsequent maintenance, much easier. And luckily, most of these tools are mostly fairly inexpensive, small and easy to store. Some of the larger and more expensive tools can generally be rented at a wide variety of locations.

When considering whether to rent or own a particular tool, ask yourself whether or not you are likely to get much use out of it beyond this present project. For example, if you are using a trencher, it is not likely that you will need it around much once you have dug your trenches, so that rental is likely a no-brainer. Same thing with a sod cutter, which of course is only used for . . . . cutting sod. Rakes, shovels, etc. are probably items that will be helpful down the road, so those I would definitely own.

Rototiller? A medium-duty rototiller perfect for loosening up that compacted clay soil in your backyard is going to run you about $60 a day from a Home Depot, or similar rental company. Not a king's ransom for a specific, useful tool, but consider. . . . .

Along the way, you are likely going to want to rototill SEVERAL times. Not only once all the weeds, dead grass and everything else in your yard has been removed, but also at least a couple of times more, as I will explain later. This being the case, it might make sense to take another approach.

Confronted with this dilemma, I chose to go out and purchase a lighter duty, but easily transportable tiller. I chose the Stihl Yard Boss. Very light and easy to operate, very dependable and sturdily built, I have literally done all the tilling I needed to on an entire 1200 square foot lawn with just this tool.

The drawbacks? Well, it is admittedly not as powerful as its larger counterparts, meaning you will likely take a bit more time on any given area on your lawn. And because its track is considerably narrower than the rental version, it will take more passes to cover the same area. I figured it would more than pay for itself in the long run and it has. I think I paid around $300 for mine, roughly 4-5 times of what it costs to rent a larger, commercial model.

But remember, I NEVER have to return I, allowing me to complete a given project at my own pace and convenience. Everyone's situation is different. Just something to consider.

THE REMOVAL OF EXISTING GRASS OR WEEDS AND SOIL PREPARATION

For the purpose of this E-book, I am going to assume that you are starting this project on a piece of land that a) has an existing water connection and hose bib already installed. (This is where your common garden hose would be connected), b) is either a lawn that has been neglected too long or is raw dirt (as opposed to concrete or brick) and c) is on a piece of land that may be on an incline, but will require no heavy duty terracing or massive movement of dirt.

This describes the vast number of lawns that have prompted their owners (or perhaps even renters) to hit their threshold and declare "Something has to be done about this".

Yes, it DOES.

Sure, it may slightly resemble a lawn, but in fact this front yard is comprised almost entirely of weeds and dead grass. It all needs to go.

REMOVAL OF EXISTING GRASS AND WEEDS

Again, chances are you starting with a piece of land that has a substantial amount of growth already taking place on it. Trouble is, this growth is almost certain to be comprised of a variety of weeds and not an actual green and thriving lawn.

The first step here is to get rid of that mixture of weeds, dead grass and whatever else that almost certainly sits on top of the space that will soon be your lawn. The most thorough and effective way to do that is by using a spray-on herbicide like Round- Up or something similar. When you choose your own product to use, make sure that you are getting something designed to kill ALL grass, and is not just a "Weed and Feed" product designed to kill specific weeds but leave the grass intact. Certainly there is a place for these products, but the idea here is total weed and grass removal.

You will almost certainly find it best to start from scratch, even in situations where some viable grass may still be visible. While you may be tempted to see if you can work around what may be a negligible amount of healthy grass already present, I can tell you from experience it will not likely be worth the extra effort it will take to keep that grass alive as you work around it. The establishment of a healthy lawn, be it through the use of seed or sod, takes place quite a bit later in the process, and in the meantime, there will be a lot of work to do – likely right where this grass is already situated.

Before starting on this step, be sure and read the product directions thoroughly. And make sure you have plenty of product in an easy to use container – NOT a spray bottle. For a yard of any size, it takes FOREVER to get the spray coverage you need to complete the job if you're using a common spray bottle.

Instead, get the larger container that features the spray-gun already attached, and comes with a pressurizer that keeps the flow of herbicide out the gun fairly constant. A container like this will generally hold about a gallon and a third, usually more than enough to cover even a fairly large amount of land. Look for a type of container labeled "Pump and Go', or something similar. It's a design that with just a few pumps on the handle will get you about five minutes of spray time. This saves a LOT of energy in the process.

Also, Roundup is a pretty efficient product. When the label says all you have to do is get the weeds wet with it, take it literally. No need to overspray - it won't kill the weeds any faster.

Here's a suggested alternative, if you are dealing with a REALLY big patch of land, is to get an all-purpose sprayer with an even larger pressurized handle, and get the Round Up concentrate to prepare your own mixture.

A larger capacity yard sprayer to the left, alongside the more compact, manufacturer-supplied applicator. If the yard you are working on is sizable, you will save yourself a lot of effort by opting for the one on the left and buying concentrate.

No matter what product you decide on, be sure and take all the necessary listed precautions. I've never had any bad reactions from using herbicides, but there's no use being careless. Make sure you applying this product on a relatively still day, as too much wind can not only make your efforts less effective and could blow a lot of that product right back at you. You don't want that. Also, make sure you wash your hands thoroughly when you come back in the house, and don't touch anyone, human or animal, until you do. Just a little common sense.

As effective as the herbicide is, it WILL take a while to work – often a few days. Just be patient and let the product take its course, even though you may be thinking to yourself "What difference does it make? All this foliage is getting removed, anyway".

It actually DOES make a difference. Products like Round Up actually travel through the weed down to its root system, so you want to give the product time to get there. Otherwise, you may remove the top of the weed and leave a viable root system below, which leaves the door open for additional weed growth in fairly short order.

There will come a point where it become obvious that the product has run its course. Any weeds or grass remnants will be very light in color, and should curl up and dry out. At this point, it will be time to move on to the next step.

GRASS REMOVAL

Now that the visible weeds and grass are now dead, you will need to remove them. There are a few ways to get this done, and ultimately the course you take should be dependent at least in part on just how much material there is to remove.

If you are dealing with a plot of land literally covered from end to end with dead grass, weeds or a mixture thereof, it will probably make sense to go out and rent a sod cutter (described earlier) from a nearby equipment rental company. As of this writing, I have found that Home Depot (www.HomeDepot.Rents.com) only sporadically carries Sod Cutters. Not sure why, really. A series of calls to them recently revealed that some locations DID keep them in stock, while others did not.

As an alternative, another home supply may carry them, or you can look in the Yellow Pages under the category of "equipment rental". I've always had good experiences with Hertz Equipment Rental (www.hertzequip.com) as well.

Whichever company you decide to go with, just a couple of pointers. For starters, any reputable equipment rental company should have people on hand that are capable AND WILLING of showing you how to safely and effectively use the piece of equipment you are renting.

Each piece of equipment necessary for this process is quite safe when used properly, but returning home with a good knowledge of how to operate the equipment is very important. It saves time once you are ready to get started (especially important, as you are likely renting by the day), so you don't want to waste time) and it certainly makes everything safer.

Be sure to familiarize yourself with all the controls on any piece you operate. For a sod cutter, you will see the obvious ignition system, fuel tank, priming pump/button, etc. and you will also see a depth adjustment that controls just how much you take 'off the top'. Think of this adjustment as something similar to beard/sideburn trimmers (but on a much grander scale), where you can control the depth of the cut.

As far as just how much to remove, there is a balance to be achieved. No need to take too much off the top, as that just wastes dirt and may leave you with a starting surface that is lower than what you want relative to your sidewalk or driveway that surrounds your lawn. It also leaves you with more material to dispose of.

On the other hand, if you adjust the control for the cut to be too shallow, you may just be mowing your lawn – more or less – and leaving the weed roots behind. Instead, as you embark on this process, check the ground UNDERS what has been cut out. If there is nothing but dirt showing, and no remaining grass or weed roots, you have the depth adjusted to where you want it to be. If, however, you see roots sticking out of the ground you've already passed over with the cutter, you'll need to adjust the depth setting.

Also, as you begin this step, you should mentally trace a path you are going to follow while removing that top layer from your yard. There is no need for more than a small bit of overlap as you make your cuts/passes. And, as you make your way through, the top layer of the area you have covered should literally be carved off what sits beneath it. Once an appreciable amount of strips has been separated from the ground, be sure and sweep them aside so that you are not trying to "cut" sod that has already been separated.

With these remnants properly swept out of the way, it will be obvious where you left off and what still remains to be cut. Working properly and methodically with even and careful passes, even a fairly sizable front yard can be completed fairly quickly.

This photo illustrates what a sod cutter can do. You'll notice that the top layer of dead grass is largely removed, with the dirt below left intact.

Again, as a cheap, but considerably more labor intensive alternative, you can use a pick to separate grass/weeds from the dirt immediately below. This is great exercise (if you are so inclined), provided that you pace yourself, avoid getting too ambitious with the pick and stop periodically to rest and catch your breath. But, make no mistake about it, this approach is NOT for everyone. It is fairly taxing. On the upside, besides burning calories, properly done it is a very thorough approach, and once you get the hang of it, you can pretty easily control just how deep a cut you are making.

Here's another way to get the same job done, using a pick instead of a sod cutter. A lot of work, but possible, nonetheless.

WHAT TO DO WITH THE REMNANTS?

Most cities sponsor recycling programs, whereby multiple receptacles are provided, allowing you to remove weeds and grass from your yard and dump them into the "Lawn Remnants" (or similarly named) container for removal.

However, if you are working on a lawn of any size, you almost certainly will run out of room this way. So, if you really want to save money on this step, your only choice may be to remove the remnants in weekly increments (though the cutting can be done all at one time, with the waste product piled in a corner of the yard).

However, you can't beat the price this way. Just make sure you are not taking too much dirt with you as you with the remnants, as this can result in your starting point being lower than the surrounding concrete or cement (not a good look) and can make those receptacles REALLY heavy to move out to the curb. Ethically as well, it would seem a good idea to keep what you toss into the receptacle to just dead grass and weeds. Those certainly qualify as 'yard remnants'. Dirt would not, and since it's pretty heavy, your local sanitation department may not be happy if they have to replace your receptacle if it cracks.

If you are okay with moving up a notch, cost-wise, you can hire a hauling service to come and remove whatever material you have gathered. Costs vary considerably if you go this route. Not long ago, I paid about $370 to have a two-person crew come and remove about 1200 square feet (i.e. a 40' x 30' yard) and haul it away. Seems a little steep, but at the time it was worth it to me to get that part out of the way so that I could continue working without much delay.

A CLEAN SLATE – It's Tilling Time

Now that the weeds/dead grass are gone, you are left with what is likely a barren-looking patch of land- likely compacted and unforgiving. It may seem almost rock-solid in texture, and only yield a slight bit after being drenched in water, which may very well just sit in a sort of sheet above the ground, and not even seem to be absorbed. Herein lies the reason why lawns, once neglected, start to go downhill pretty fast.

If you were to simply try and place seed or sod on top of this, you may well get some of it to germinate or grow. Maybe not, though. In fairly short order, the grass would begin to wither and die. The growth of its root base would soon exceed the ability of water and nutrients to get deep enough to keep things alive.

This is a sort of snapshot of what goes wrong with improperly prepared soil even when a lawn is already present. The presence of mostly clay soil makes it almost impossible for water and nutrients to make their way to the root of the grass (or plants, in the case of flowerbeds). Clay soil will only grudgingly take in water, and once it does, and since it also tends to drain improperly, it also quickly gives rise to mildew, which will inhibit plant growth. When it does dry, the soil becomes rock-hard, and in effect, strangles the roots.

Bottom line. . . if you have clay soil and you want to end up with a lawn you can be proud of, you WILL have to alter its composition.

So . . . What to Do?

The short answer is . . . get the soil loosened up (hopefully on a long term basis, though this will take more effort down the road) to the point where nutrients and water will pass through the top layer of dirt, instead of merely sitting on top of it. This will help your lawn to thrive.

While there are a number of products out there that CLAIM to loosen up clay soil, some purporting to work by merely spraying ON TOP of the existing soil and not even requiring to be mixed or tilled into the soil, I have found that a more 'low-tech' approach works best when you are first establishing viable soil for your lawn.

I use gypsum. Otherwise known by its more formal name, calcium sulfate. When properly mixed into existing soil, no matter how bad off the soil is, gypsum doesn't so much alter the chemical structure of the soil, but rather mixes with it to keep it from compacting. Just how much gypsum will you need? Well, that actually depends on how bad off your soil is to start with. Have a look at the photos that accompany this part of the process and you will see that I use a SUBSTANTIAL amount of the stuff to get it to work. Maybe 1-2 bags for every 12-16 square feet. Good thing it's not very expensive.

While it may be tempting to try and skip this step, and go right into mixing soil conditioner or fertilizer into your existing yard, you'll find that most soil conditioners (like "Amend", for example) do not contain a sufficient amount of gypsum to really transform soil that is bad off to begin with.

Depending on where you live, and your proximity to home improvement stores, you may also find that, if you are working on a large yard, the price of those bags of Amend (or similar product) tend to add up. While $5 to $6 a bag may not seem like a lot, multiply that by the 30 or 40 bags you may need for an appreciably sized yard, and you start to get the picture.

A cost saving solution that has consistently worked well for me is to substitute a combination of steer manure and the aforementioned gypsum in a proportion of about 3 bags of steer manure (at one cubic foot per bag) – with one bag of gypsum.

Since, as of this writing, the gypsum generally costs about $2.50 a bag and the steer manure a mere 85-90 cents per bag, a mixture of the two equal to one bag of your brand name soil conditioner (which generally comes in 2 cubic foot bags) will average out to more like $3.00 as opposed to $5 or $6.

If your yard is not particularly sizable, the savings may not be worth pursuing, as products like Amend certainly do what they advertise, but if you are working with a big yard the savings can add up.

You may not be sure if the soil you are working with requires all this work? It may not. Though it's been my experience that far more yards tend to be comprised of predominately clay, compacted soil than the opposite (sandy soil), your situation may vary. Besides, there really is no downside to having an optimally fertilized and prepped lawn.

An easy way to determine where you stand in this regard is to thoroughly wet a patch of dirt (maybe a foot square), let the water settle in, and then grab a handful of it.

If you squeeze the dirt, then release it and it stays in one piece, you have a clay soil issue to deal with. If the dirt simply crumbles apart and falls to the ground, then you likely have no worries, and can instead get started building up the nutrient content in the soil.

You can see the gypsum already spread across the ground, as indicated by the off white powder. The bags of steer manure have been placed, so that they are evenly distributed across the area to be worked on.

To enhance the effectiveness of this step, instead of just spreading gypsum on top of the dirt, you'll want wet the dirt a little to keep the dust to a minimum and rototill the gypsum/steer manure combination (or Amend, if you so choose) THOROUGHLY into the existing dirt. It's more work this way, but the results are worth the trouble. Applying future treatments of gypsum on top of the lawn periodically can help keep the soil from compacting, providing it is done with sufficient quantities and repeatedly watered into the soil.

Without moving the bags, they are then split open and emptied,
leaving their contents right where we want them.

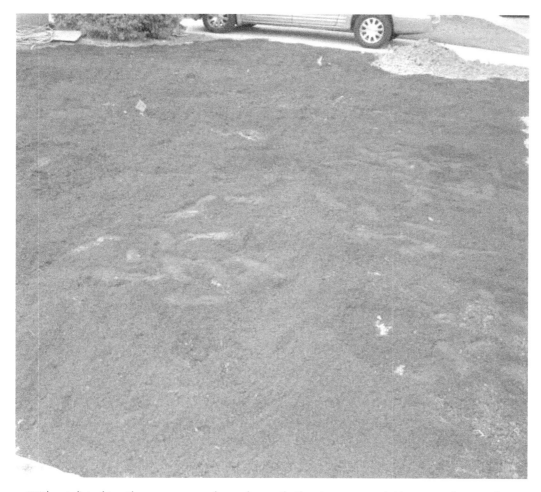

Without disturbing the gypsum powder underneath, the steer manure is then spread out so that, once rototilled, it will be evenly distributed into the soil.

During this process, you'll want to try to till in straight rows, with a little bit of overlap between them. Also, try and keep track of where last left off when starting a new row. Use the rototiller as you would a lawn mower – working in straight, slightly overlapping rows. This step may sound like a very easy task, but when you combine the shifting of dirt caused by the rototiller with plain old fashioned human error, it's easy to lose track of where you last left off. The back and forth action of the rototiller causes small undulations in the dirt, and if you are not paying attention, you can create low and high spots in your once level yard. Some portions of your yard end up THOROUGHLY tilled, while others areas are not tilled at all, as you will find once the area has been leveled with a rake. Doesn't seem like a big deal, but it is.

To avoid this, I would recommend taking a fairly manageable area of the yard to be planted, maybe 200-300 square feet (the length and width will of course vary with the shape of your yard) and concentrate on getting this area mixed evenly. With a smaller segment to work with, there is less chance for the dirt to be redistributed unevenly. You can mark off the area to be worked on with police tape or cones to mark where you left off.

In order to redistribute relatively small amounts of dirt once you have things more or less level, you can use a straight board dragged across the surface, as shown here.

It makes things a little more manageable to work a yard in sections. Here, we can see the first section, approximately 8' x 30', with steer manure rototilled in. It was then levelled using a level board and a hose to get things to settle.

A second section is completed, using the same methodology.

Working from one end to the other, the yard is completed in this manner. The jacaranda leaves will have to go before the final steps.

Breaking this process up into manageable parts will also give you a tangible sense of accomplishment and will help ensure that each section folds into the section after it, leaving no obvious demarcation between areas you've worked on.

So, as you complete this portion of the process, make sure you stop periodically and get your visual bearings. Make sure that you have been tilling at a fairly uniform depth, and have not merely been going over the same small area of dirt continuously.

As an alternative to this, merely stop tilling every so often, grab a rake and level the area you have been working on. You will find that a rototiller will leave dirt behind it, as well as to the sides and even in front. Leveling the area will you keep track of where you need to get to next.

For each section you rototill, it is a good idea to move through it in both directions - both latitudinal and longitudinally - for best results. Then, after doing so, you will want to go back through with a heavy duty rake and get everything level again. I generally make it a point to level the area I've most recently been working on before quitting for the day. It helps keep the surface of each area consistent and gives you a good feeling of accomplishment.

You will eventually reach a point where you have achieved a nice, even, relatively level surface throughout the entire yard. It's always a good idea to double check just how level everything is from a variety of perspectives, as surrounding fencing and foliage can alter your perception of just how level everything is.

So, be sure and inspect the area you are working on – again, both latitudinally and longitudinally, to see if there are any high points or low points. You can also turn on a garden hose and begin to saturate the area you worked on. If the area is uneven, after a few minutes you'll begin to see water pool at the low points.

Also, don't neglect the areas upon which you plan on placing flowerbeds and concentrate solely on the lawn. Now is a good time to till those areas as well. The looser and better conditioned the soil, the easier it is to get plant life to grow. In most cases, flowerbeds are elevated somewhat above the level of the lawn, so you will want to plan accordingly as far as how much soil conditioner or gypsum/steer manure and additional soil you put down there.

Once you have gone through your entire yard in this manner, with all the individual sections worked over and then levelled to make sure they match the sections alongside, you should be left with a nice, level yard that now looks markedly more fertile (and darker) than what you started with.

You now have a nice clean slate to work with, so it's time to start creating.

PLANNING OUT YOUR SYSTEM, INCLUDING CREATING A SHOPPING LIST OF MATERIALS AND SUPPLIES

PLANNING THINGS OUT

Before you get started digging, you'll certainly need to have a thorough idea of what you want your finished yard area to look like. . . . . . What shape will the lawn be? Where are you positioning your flowerbeds? Etc.

Rarely will your first shot at this be the vision you stick with.

Among the factors you should consider . . .

How much maintenance are you willing to do? Some lawns are more delicate than others. I generally work with fescue, and find it pretty hardy, though not overly drought tolerant. A sports field is generally comprised of Bermuda, also pretty sturdy stuff. In contrast, there are certain ornamental lawns that are *very* delicate. They may look nice, but you do need to ask yourself if you are willing to put in the extra effort and expense to maintain a more delicate lawn. Probably not. Any lawn requires upkeep. That is a given. But you would do well to consider installing a grass type that is appropriate for your geography and the amount of time and effort you are willing to put in.

You've likely already spent at least a little time considering what you want your finished work to look like- considered whether or not you will want flower beds bordering your lawn, where those flower beds might be situated, or maybe you have opted to just go with wall to wall grass. Hopefully at this point you have also considered where the shade hits for a good part of the year. And no doubt you have long since identified just where the water source that will power this whole system is located. The design portion is a fun and rewarding part of the process, and the time you spend on it really pays dividends in the form of the finished product.

A couple of other considerations:

If you are picturing your yard as having a lot of variation in height, slope, etc., but do not currently have the dirt in place to work with, are you really willing to do what is necessary to either rent grading equipment or have someone grade the land for you?

Does the land you are working with feature a tree or trees that will create an issue with the lawn receiving enough sunlight during certain seasons? If so, you'll need to plan for this. Your chosen lawn species will need to be able to handle prolonged shade, and you probably will need to make some arrangements to at least occasionally get the tree or trees thinned out so that enough light reaches the grass. Even the most shade-resistant varieties of grass need **some** exposure to the sun.

You can use existing sidewalks, pathways, or any other permanent concrete or stone features that will remain in place as a sort of visual reference point for the overall slope of your lawn-to-be. In other words, if your yard will be bordering a sidewalk that you plan on keeping in place, (assuming we are not talking about a public sidewalk, which MUST stay in place), and that sidewalk features a slight downward grade from front to back, it will make visual sense to also make sure the dirt adjacent to that sidewalk follows pretty much the same angle, so that ultimately your lawn does the same.

TIME TO CREATE

Not possessing much in the way of freehand drawing skills, so when I set about to design a layout, I generally use either graph paper or a software program like PhotoImpact (a more primitive and cheaper cousin of Photoshop), so that I will have some built in assistance as far as straight lines are concerned. Should you not already have a drawing program on your computer (PhotoImpact, or something similar) I've also found that "graph paper"- paper stock that features nothing but squares throughout – both up and down and sideways, will also work as a substitute.

If you decide on the latter, to keep your distances between sprinklers, landmarks, sidewalks, etc. in proportion, all you have to do is count out how many squares run in each direction and write it down. Then, go out to your yard with a tape measure and get overall measurements in both directions. Once you have this information, you can then come up with a number value for distance that each square will have.

For example, let's say your lawn measures 20' x 30', and that pad of graph paper in front of you features 40 squares vertically and 30 squares across (just an example). Well, then your work is pretty easy for this step – each square will then represent one square foot and you will draw out the perimeter of your lawn using 20 of the available 30 squares across, and 30 of the 40 available squares vertically.

It's always a good idea to have some room OUTSIDE the perimeter of the sketch of your yard, as you will want to be fairly accurate in drawing in the location of your water source, sidewalks, flowerbed, etc. This will be your de facto starting point when you design your system.

Now, it's time to get creative.

SOME POINTS TO PONDER:

As you create your drawing (or schematic) - of the total space available, as represented on the page, how much is going to be actual lawn, and how much flowerbed? You are going to want to draw that in – again using caution (either visually with the software program, or with proper use of the squares on the graph paper as a reference point) to keep everything to scale.

Will the flowerbed have a straight border or a curved one? Draw it in, again doing your best to keep everything to scale.

Do you intend to put a vegetable garden out there somewhere? Go ahead and put that in there too, but be sure to mark it so that it can easily be differentiated from your other flowerbeds, even if it is very close to where the rest of the flowerbed may be, because a vegetable garden has different irrigation needs that will be accommodated. More on this later.

On the accompanying pages you will see some example sketches of how this process might go, using a design based on an actual backyard. While the artwork may be far from inspired, it should give you a pretty good idea as to how to go about this process.

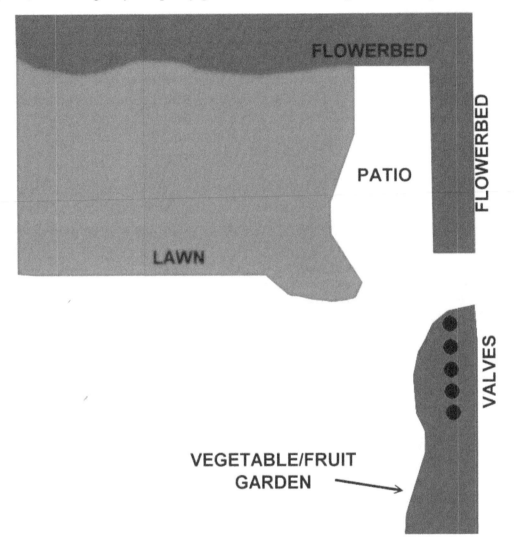

While not including the actual trees and flowers that are already situated, this PhotoImpact rendering shows the layout of the yard we will be working with before any irrigation goes in.

One thing you will want to avoid right off is to route the system in a single sequence from one end to another. You will see in the next Illustration what I mean. Instead of designing the flow through the pipes in a series of intersecting branches, it is a common mistake to simply connect up to the manifold (more on manifolds later) and run PVC pipe in a continuous loop through your yard.

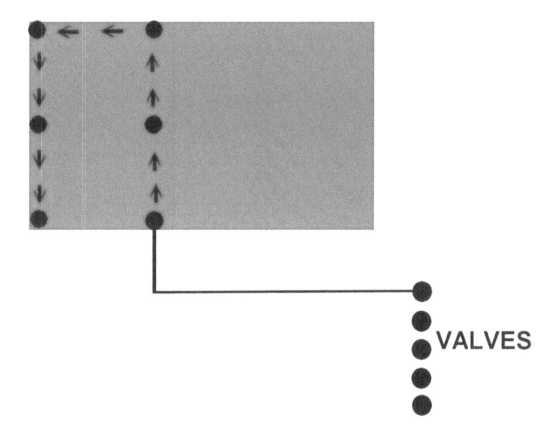

This yields an inferior result. The biggest problem with this approach is that you will lose water pressure after each sprinkler, as the sprinkler, in effect, releases pressure from the system. By the time you get to the last sprinkler in the series, you are only left with a fraction of the water pressure you started with, so that very last sprinkler, which would otherwise cover say a 10-foot radius, is actually only capable of getting the water out to 7-8 feet. This will result in areas of the lawn that have insufficient coverage, leading to dead spots over time.

Instead, you will want to make sure you design your own system so that each of the sprinklers is receiving more or less the same amount of water flow, as shown immediately following:

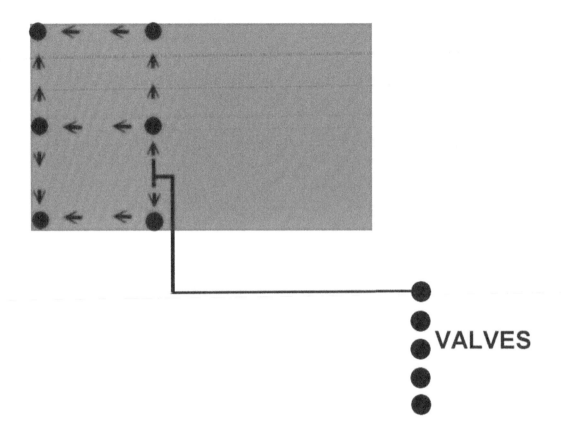

VALVES

If you feel your design skills leave something to be desired, or you simply want a more professional input into your design, another route you can go on this is to have such a design generated professionally and ***often at no charge***. For example, Rain Bird, a leading manufacturer of irrigation parts, is one of several free sources intended to help a homeowner design his or her system.

You can find out more at http://www.rainbird.com. Just go to their page, go to the "Homeowners" tab, and then to "Get a Sprinkler Design for Your Yard". You will be asked to provide some dimensions on your yard, as well as a rough sketch on the graph paper they supply. Once completed to the best of your ability, you submit your sketch to them and within 10 days, they will respond back with both a sketch showing what they deem to be the best design for your yard's system, as well as a parts list that will show everything required. Like most things, you should double-check their work as well before taking it as gospel, but it will, most of the time, be surprisingly accurate and relevant (though only as good and accurate as the information you initially supply ***them***). The shopping list is a BIG help, as it will allow you to walk into your local home improvement store, ready to load items into your cart, as opposed the more laborious process of tallying what quantities of each part your sketch called for.

This is actually a pretty big time saver.

SOME OF THE PARTS/ITEMS YOU WILL BE WORKING WITH:

Stations

Your irrigation system will be comprised of several **stations** (from 1 to perhaps 6, depending on how elaborate and varied your final design is). Simply put, a station is a group of sprinklers powered by the same valve that operate in unison. The location of these sprinklers is only part of the equation in what ties them together. PURPOSE is much more important than proximity. In other words, if you were to take 8 sprinklers and tie them together to make a single station, their purpose (WHAT they are irrigating) is much more important than WHERE they are irrigating.

You don't want to add stations unnecessarily, as it just adds labor, but on the other hand, you don't want to try and save time by connecting a group of sprinklers to the same valve ONLY because they are in the same area.

Manifold

Originating where you (or more likely your plumber) attaches a copper "T" fitting to your water source at the hose bib, a manifold is actually the de facto 'heart' of your irrigation system. It is made up of the individual valves that power the aforementioned stations, conveniently grouped together in one place, with the valves wired to your timer.

This photo shows the rear portion of a manifold installed. The ground below had been excavated so that it could be positioned properly, then backfilled and levelled so that the manifold is sitting on solid ground. To the immediate right, you can also see how the manifold is connected to the T fitting.

TYING IT ALL TOGETHER IN A DESIGN

So just to reiterate, as you design your system, I would recommend that you group your sprinklers into a station based on their purpose – WHAT they will be irrigating and how much sunlight the area gets, as opposed to their location.

With some exceptions, lawns generally require more water than plants, so plan accordingly. I wouldn't recommend designing your system so that sprinklers meant for lawn irrigation are covering the needs or plants or other foliage. Also, if a portion of a given area receives a lot more shade during the course of the day, it will need substantially less water, as that area may eventually mildew if it is saturated too frequently and not allowed to drain.

One factor that will determine just how many sprinklers you can connect to one station (and therefore, how many stations you'll ultimately need) is the amount of water flow and water pressure you have at your disposal. These are very important factors to take into consideration in the design process.

Too little available flow will mean that you can only group a small number of sprinklers together to work in unison, and you will therefore need more STATIONS to accomplish your goal of an effective irrigation system.

In some cases, (a very small yard, for example) this doesn't matter much. With less square footage to be accounted for, how many sprinklers you'll ultimately use is not a big deal

But on the other end of the scale, it is important to point out that most readily available RESIDENTIAL timers (Orbit, Rain Bird, etc.) max out at 9 stations or so. And even though 9 stations are a lot to account for in the case of most houses, if your water is just trickling out of the water source to such an extent that you can only put 2-3 sprinklers on a station, this total can get eaten up pretty quickly. Unusual, but possible. With proper water flow and water pressure, to put things in perspective, on an approximately 30' x 40' parcel of land that includes mostly lawn, but also shrubs lining a 20' walkway and two separate rose beds, I used a total of 6 stations connected to a 6 station timer, and could have gotten away with maybe one fewer station.

The more stations you need, the more ditches need to be dug, the more PVC pipe needs to be laid, the more sprinklers need to be connected. None of it a particularly distasteful or difficult task, but why do any more than you have to?

FIGURING THE PRESSURE OF YOUR WATER SYSTEM

In order to properly design your system, you are going to need to know (most importantly) the available water *flow* you will have at your disposal to "power the sprinklers". After all, every component you are going to be using is going to be dependent on adequate water pressure to work properly. If you were to examine a sprinkler and determine its "range" (the amount of distance it should be able to spray water), you'll find it pretty readily on its seal. Just bear in mind that this figure is based on the availability of *adequate* water pressure, available in a reasonable amount of flow. So, while a given sprinkler may sport a label showing its effective range is 12' it's not going to get there if the water flow is sub-par.

At first glance, these two measurements (water *flow* and water *pressure*) may seem to be one and the same. But they are not. Think about it. When you place your thumb or finger over a hose to increase its force, you are also increasing the effective pressure of the spray. However, you're doing nothing to increase the flow coming out of the hose. A pipe that is filled with corrosion may also increase the pressure when measured at the pipe's end. But again, the flow is not going to be elevated at all.

The best (and easiest) way to determine your available flow is to simply go out and get a 5-gallon bucket, and see how long it takes to fill up with the water turned on full bore. But with one catch.

In order to do this part accurately, you would ideally want to measure this flow not from the hose bib itself, but rather at the end of the first 90 degree fitting that is installed. Or rather, WILL be installed.

A close up shot of the T-fitting (professionally installed), along with the threaded male adapter and other PVC fittings used to connect the manifold. As you can see, a separate shut-off valve is also added. This comes in handy if you want to work on the system at a later date without having to shut off water to the entire house. The shutoff valve to the entire house can be seen at the lower right. If you notice where the threaded male adapter is situated, that is where you would insert the pressure gauge to get an applicable reading.

Measuring the available flow will require you to get water from an unrestricted spot. What this means is that you must measure directly from the output of your water pump right after the first 90-degree fitting, not from the hose bib itself. Simply time how long it takes to fill a 5-gallon bucket full. If you fill it in 15 seconds, then you have 20 (5 gallons x 1 minute (the 15 seconds x 4) gallons per minute available to work with. To get a more accurate reading, you will want to get the water going full force before placing the bucket underneath it.

To measure water pressure, you can get a ***pressure gauge*** with ***a hose bib adapter from most home improvement stores.*** (Water pressure you should measure right from the hose bib). After the gauge is screwed on, just turn on the water supply and read what the PSI is. You'll want at least 40 psi, and no more than 75 psi for a residential sprinkler design.

SOME OF THE REASONS WHY YOUR FLOW MAY BE LESS THAN IT SHOULD BE:

Small diameter pipe was used in this area –Many old houses feature a small (maybe ¾"in diameter) t- junction that comes off the main pipe near the hose bib. This design often wreaks havoc with the flow available to an otherwise viable system. By how much? Often as much as half, meaning you may only get six feet of range from a sprinkler otherwise rated at 12' feet of throw. If you are going to try to power your sprinkler system under these circumstances, be prepared to place a lot of sprinklers and a lot of stations. You'll need them.

A relatively inexpensive solution, rather than adding countless stations and sprinklers, would be to get a plumber to connect a sort of "override" to this part of your water system, so that you are able to use a larger diameter pipe all the way through to the end of the system. The accompany photo below shows one way to solve this problem – by installing larger diameter pipe in the area.

Here's an override. This fitting, coming out from under the house, was installed so that the relatively small diameter pipe (vertical portion partially seen) could be bypassed to enhance water flower. It connects to the vertical fitting at the left, indicated by the bluish shutoff valve.

Corrosion – Over time, sediment and corrosion can build up in any pipe. Eventually, a pipe that was meant to provide a ½" of diameter and abundant water flow progressively loses some of its circumference. Again, this may actually INCREASE the available pressure, but the actual flow will be reduced.

For simplicity's sake, we'll assume that you can get the necessary 15-20 gph necessary to run an appreciable number of sprinklers at the same time.

(If this is not actually the case, then one of the two causes listed above is almost certainly to blame, and the only way to remedy the situation would be to enlist the services of a plumber. No one likes to spend any more money than necessary on household repairs, but this is far from a major repair and can be accomplished by a skilled professionally fairly quickly.

So, back to that flow of 20gpm (gallons per minute). Where will that get you as far as designing and constructing a sprinkler system? Pretty far, actually. Let's just use a typical sprinkler (non-rotor type) as a reference point. It will require water pressure of at least 15 psi and flow of .1 gpm to work. Not to work optimally, just to work at all. But look at this a little closer, and you will see that this really should present no problem.

Let's say you have 8 sprinklers running off one station. Well, using that figure of 20 gallons per minute (gpm) divided by the 8 sprinklers that will be pulling water at the same time leaves you an average of 2.5 gpm per sprinkler. Literally 25 times the minimum needed to activate the sprinkler. You really should have no worries. Even 10 sprinklers running at the same time would be no issue. Unless you are working on a VERY big plot of land, you can make a lot of progress on irrigating your lawn with 8-10 sprinklers operating at the same time.

I wouldn't recommend, however, trying to max out the number of sprinklers connected to a single valve to the extent that every fraction of gpm is accounted for. When you stretch the available supply so thin, even a subtle variation in water pressure can cause the sprinklers in the station to operate at less than optimal flow. Enough variations in water pressure and before too long before you started to see some dry spots on your lawn from where the water didn't quite get to where it needed to go.

Most residential sprinklers are rated for a range (spacing) of 3ft to 20ft. You want head to head coverage, meaning that the outer reaches of the spray from the first sprinkler should easily be hitting the head of the sprinkler closest to it. This way, if a wind kicks up, or water flow is somehow reduced (say, by the use of a nearby hose to wash the car) etc., you still have the coverage you need to get the job done.

Be sure and resist another temptation to cut corners by spacing your sprinklers further apart (thus requiring fewer of them) and relying on a slight overlap between them to count on adequate coverage. It won't work nearly as well. Same reason as above.

Those first 2 rows of 4 sprinklers across you see in the illustration are covering a lawn that is about 40 feet wide. This means that they are spaced about 10 feet from each other, plenty close enough to ensure optimal sprinkler head to sprinkler head coverage without having to use unnecessary sprinklers. As the lawn tapers along the walkway, you will see that fewer sprinklers are relied on, and about the same amount of spacing is used.

COMPLETING YOUR PLAN

By methodically placing your sprinklers (be they lawn sprinklers or shrub sprinklers for plants) where they need to go to fulfill your design and to maintain proper (HEAD TO HEAD) coverage, you should be able to move through the entire yard, station by station, until everything is accounted for. Below is a station by station schematic showing each station (and its sprinklers) being added on top of the one before it. This sequence is based on an actual yard.

Just a PVC recap. The black circles in the following drawings represent the sprinklers themselves. Solid black lines represent PVC pipe. Wherever you see the two directly connected, it means either a threaded "T" or a threaded elbow (both with a ½" opening to accommodate a sprinkler riser), depending on whether the sprinkler sits in between two pipes joined together or at the very end of a pipe. Wherever you see one PVC pipe connected just to the side of a sprinkler, it would denote the use of an unthreaded "T" (because no sprinkler riser is being used).

Also, in the case of this yard, most of the concrete around the patio was poured AFTER the system was created. For those of you dealing with existing concrete already in place, you would want to try and tunnel under the shortest expanse of concrete possible (generally 3-4 feet is not that difficult), as opposed to running more or less perpendicular to the manifold, as shown in these illustrations.

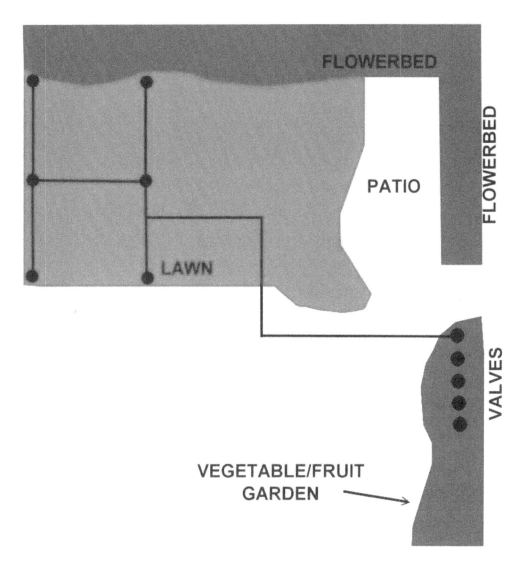

As you can tell from the graphic above, station 1 extends to the farthest portion of the yard, services that part of the lawn, and is comprised of six sprinklers. Note how the locations of the sprinklers (also indicated by the black circles on the lawn itself) have been determined for head to head coverage and will not exceed the recommend range of the sprinklers being used.

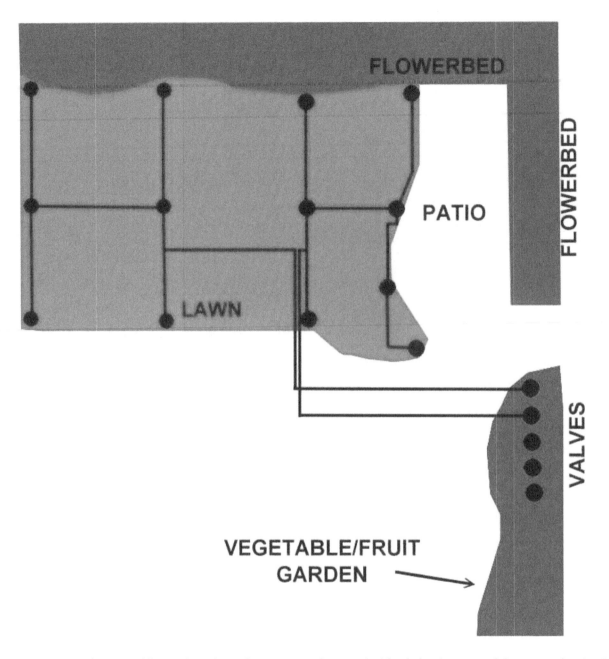

Station 2 will service the other (approximate) half of the lawn and is comprised of seven sprinklers. Same concept as far as their placement. The only real difference is that, because of the curvature of the lawn adjacent to the patio, some slight re-routing of the PVC pipe has to be done. For purposes of this drawing and on the actual job, PVC elbows are used to bring the pipe in/out so that the sprinkler head can be positioned optimally, just a couple of inches in from the patio itself. You can accomplish this same thing with flexible PVC hosing, which can join two rigid PVC pipes and is usually available in the same section as other PVC fittings.

Of note also is the positioning of some of the PVC pipe for this station, adjacent to the existing pipes that are in use for Station One and run across the lawn. A wider trench was created for this purpose, which though requiring a bit of extra work, is still easier than digging another entirely separate trench for the same use.

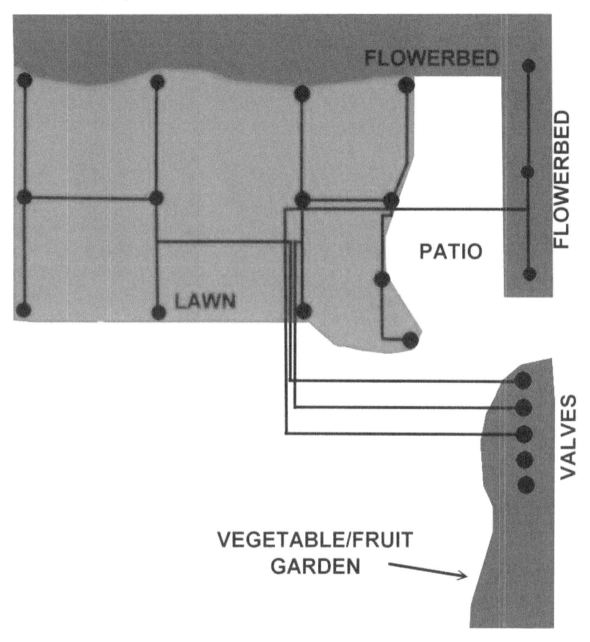

Station 3 will service a flower bed that is west facing and is immediately adjacent to the west side of a house. I mention both of these factors because they play a part in the design of this system. The fact that this area is west facing means that it will only receive direct sunlight in the later part of the day, and the fact that it is adjacent to the house would mean that you'd want to consider a different type of irrigation than regular shrub sprinklers, so as to save some unneeded exposure of the house to direct spray. The same trench that accommodates some of the PVC piping for Stations One and Two also contains the PVC pipe for Station Three that runs across the yard in the same location. The drawing may make it seem that a wide trench will be necessary but, considering the PVC pipe itself is only ¾" wide and that two lengths of pipe can sit side by side, in reality not that much space is needed.

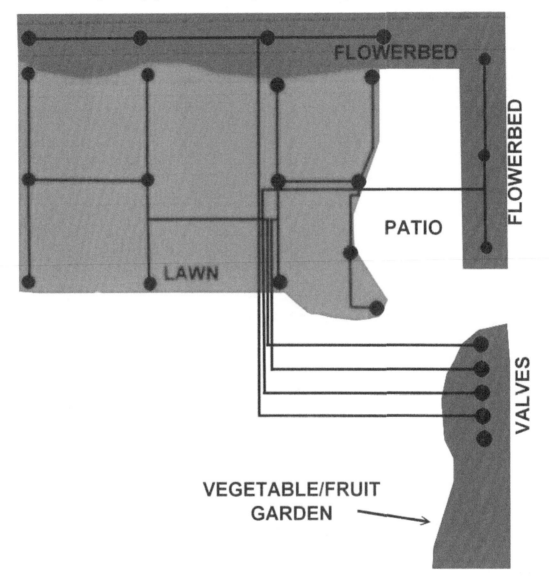

Station 4 also services a flower bed, but faces south (meaning more exposure to sunlight during any given day) and borders a cinder block wall, as opposed to a house (meaning that direct water spray from shrub sprinklers is far less of an issue). As you can see, the same trench is used again here.

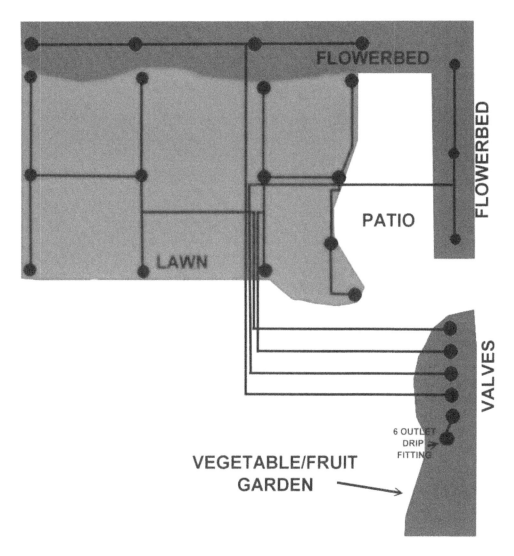

Station 5 services a vegetable garden. These generally do best with DRIP irrigation (more on that shortly) as opposed to direct spray. Tomato plants and other varieties in particular are prone to mildew if condensation from sprinklers (or even climatic conditions) tend to stay on the leaves for too long. Rose bushes are the same way and also do better with either DRIP irrigation or the use of a soaker hose, a black hose with perforations so that water slowly leaks out and onto the adjacent ground.

The sequence above was meant as an example. Of course, any individual yard is going to vary somewhat from this, and you should plan accordingly. And along the way, there will be some permissible variations, of course. If the watering needs of adjacent types of plants are similar, but one type does better with drip irrigation while the others do better with getting some water on their actual leaves (which in some cases cools things for more optimal conditions) there is no big problem with mixing the two, as long as this is properly planned for.

For example, if necessary, you can easily convert a riser that would otherwise be used for a standard shrub sprinkler into a source for a drip system by using the proper connection, as shown immediately below.

At the left you can see a standard sprinkler riser adapted for drip irrigation. The "L" shaped adapter fits into a coupler that, in turn, holds the actual tubing in place. At the right, you can see an expanse of this tubing, with a button dripper attached

For the most part, if you are planning on putting in some flowerbeds, you will want to make sure that those are properly accounted for, and accounted for on a station SEPARATE from the one that services a lawn that may be right next to it. The lawn will generally need more water than the flowerbed, unless the latter is receiving appreciably more sunlight.

A BRIEF OVERVIEW OF SOME OF THE IRRIGATION PRODUCTS AT YOUR DISPOSAL

As you go through your planning, it may help to go over some of the more common irrigation products (both as far as their patterns and their purpose) readily available along the way.

Quarter circle patterns are generally used for the corners of a more or less rectangular lawn.

Half circle patterns are placed on the edge of a rectangular lawn, and are meant to irrigate that half circle FORWARD, while leaving the area behind the sprinkler – likely a sidewalk or flowerbed, unirrigated except for some inevitable overspray the wind may blow backward.

Full circle patterns are used further into the interior of the lawn, and literally provide a circular coverage that should not vary in diameter as they are positioned so that the further reaches of the spray hit the head next to it.

Adjustable pattern heads are just what the name implies. These can be adjusted to spray everything from a wedge of no more than a few degrees to a full circle. Very handy to have on hand for irregularly shaped lawns as well.

Besides the complete sprinklers listed above, there are other adjustable and pre-set nozzles that can be fitted into a sprinkler body – that plastic cylinder that houses the nozzle and attaches to the irrigation pipe, that can be either fitted on an empty sprinkler body that can be purchased that way, or retrofitted onto and in place of, the existing nozzle that came with it.

These additional patterns include the same full circle, half circle, quarter circle and adjustable varieties that come with complete sprinklers, but there are also ¾, 1/3, 2/3, end strip, center strip, side strip and square patterns.

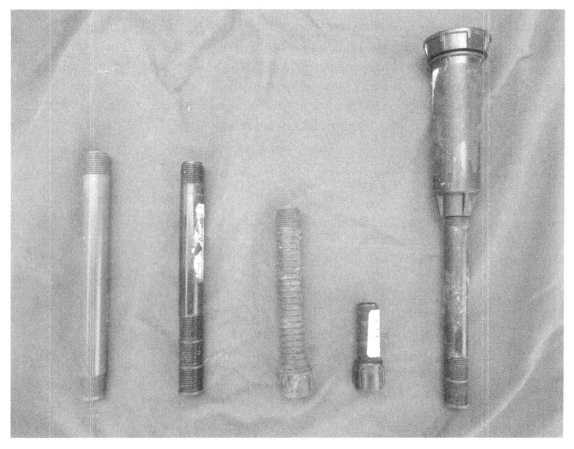

A variety of sprinkler risers. From the left to right, a solid riser (generally used for shrubs), a cutoff riser (adjust its height by cutting off threaded sections), two varieties of flexible riser (used where they may get some contact) and a sprinkler body attached to a cutoff riser for reference.

With all these variations to choose from, it should be no problem properly planning out coverage for your project. When in doubt about a specific location and the circular pattern it may need, opt for an adjustable pattern. That irregular corner that looks ALMOST like a ¾ pattern would provide adequate coverage may turn out to be more than 270 degrees. And if it is, you will end up with some dry spots if you stick with the ¾ pattern. Same goes for certain situations as far as the other fixed patterns as well.

Adjustable pattern supplies, both the complete sprinklers and nozzles, cost a little more, but it's worth having that kind of margin for error. An adjustable nozzle can always act as a ¼, ½ or even full circle pattern, but the opposite is, of course, not true.

The square, center strip, end strip and side strip varieties are designed for placement on a square plot of land (in the case of the square pattern, of course) or a rectangle (in the case of most of the others). These varieties are literally designed to spray water in a pattern that will provide deeper coverage back to front than side to side.

WHAT ABOUT FLOWERBEDS?
Pretty much everything said about lawn sprinkler varieties also holds true for flowerbed irrigation as well. Flowerbed (or shrubbery) nozzles are generally sold as nozzles only, without the accompanying bodies that you get when you buy lawn sprinklers. The nozzles attach onto risers via threaded ends on both the riser and the nozzle. The risers themselves vary in height (generally everything from 12" to 36" are readily available), and are designed not only to house the nozzle, but to give it some elevation so that the spray can get up and over the foliage that may be immediately beside it.

A shrub sprinkler in action atop a riser.

So, you can use the same nozzle patterns available for your lawn to get the coverage you need for your flowerbeds as well. The only difference, as noted, as that these nozzles will screw onto risers, instead of being housed in a sprinkler body. There are certain varieties of plants (roses or vegetable plants of any kind) that will not do well with this approach and instead require one of the following methods to grow optimally.

OTHER VARIETIES OF IRRIGATION FITTINGS

The two photos above show different uses for a button dripper. In the top photo, the dripper is attached to tubing by perforating the tubing with a punch before insertion. In the bottom photo, the dripper is inserted into micro-tubing and sits atop a riser, used to water a tomato plant.

Drippers – These are generally used for situations where it is better to water the ground around a plant than to saturate the plant itself- as with tomato plants, where getting too much water directly onto its leaves may result in mildew. An example of this would be for watering tomato plants. The use of drippers allows a slow flow of water directed at the root of the plant, keeping the moisture, and resultant mildew, off of the leaves.

Drippers are generally either mounted on small risers (micro-tubing or plastic stands that give them clearance off the ground) or are inserted directly into irrigation tubing, usually ½" in diameter. The fittings are "barbed", so the pressure of the water coming through them will not literally blow them out of position. All that is needed to insert them into the tubing is a simple punch, available at virtually any location that sells lawn supplies.

They generally come in two different varieties - flag drippers and button drippers. Essentially, they both serve the same function. I have found button drippers to be a bit sturdier, but also maybe a little more prone to clogging. Flag drippers often come apart under even minimal water pressure and need to be replaced more often.

A mushroom bubbler in action. As you can see, this piece gets its name from the spray configuration it creates, which resembles a mushroom.

'Mushroom' Bubblers- Getting their name from the mushroom-shaped pattern they emit, these are generally used for flowerbeds adjacent to walkways, where a fairly finite amount of coverage is needed. Their advantage is NOT that they keep the water off the plant – as in the case with drippers – but rather that you will not get overspray into areas you don't need.

OTHER DRIP IRRIGATION

Go to nearly any home improvement store's lawn center, and you will find quite a variety of fairly specialized drip irrigation parts. Micro-tubing to create a virtual network of drippers. Micro-sprayers to mist a pre-determined circumference with minimal water usage. And on and on. Nearly every one of these parts has its specifications listed right there on the package – water needs (expressed in Gallons Per Hour (GPH), and the circumference (where applicable), that part is capable of covering.

A word of caution about fitment (not just for sprinklers, but for the whole system)

There are relatively few manufacturers of a wide variety of lawn irrigation products – Rain Bird and Orbit, for example. Their parts are most often NOT interchangeable (with some exceptions), so it's a good idea to make sure the home improvement stores in your area carry a complete line of one or the other brand before making your choice. Valves of one brand can be combined with sprinklers of a different brand because the PVC parts and apparatus that connects the sprinklers are generally generic and will fit any brand. Always check for yourself on this, though.

I have no affiliation with any particular brand, so I also have no axe to grind. I've found Rain Bird's customer support and customer service to be outstanding. Their parts are generally very reliable, but nearly anything wears out . . .eventually, and lawn irrigation parts are not an exception.

On one occasion, when a sprinkler valve I had purchased had a solenoid that wore out *prematurely* (in Rain Bird's own estimation), they sent me a brand new one, free of charge, and OVERNIGHTED. They could have easily made the argument that, after a year or so, the valve could have just seen too much use. They didn't. On the contrary, the customer service rep I dealt with seemed almost embarrassed that the part had worn out. Literally two days later, free of charge, an entire valve arrived at my doorstep.

Pretty impressive, actually.

On the other hand, a couple of years back Rain Bird changed the configuration of its anti-siphon valves (the type you will be using) so that it became impossible to get replacement parts for any malfunctioning valve. This meant that you would end up replacing the ENTIRE valve – not a big deal financially, other than the fact that the new valves are larger than the old variety, meaning retro-fitting the new variety would also require a veritable patchwork of additional PVC parts to fit properly (and end up looking somewhat like those Habitrails you can buy for hamsters and other rodents).

Oddly, the competing brand's (Orbit's) anti-siphon valve was a direct fit for the replaced Rain Bird valve? Go figure. And I will say that one additional nice feature of the Orbit valve is that the solenoid (the portion that will be wired to your sprinkler timer) can more easily be turned on and off MANUALLY. This is great for quickly checking a particular sprinkler or station without having to go in the house and turn on the timer. Whereby the Rain Bird solenoid requires you to twist the solenoid open and shut to work manually, the Orbit model has a small, more easily operated plastic switch to the side. Over time, the twist method gets more difficult as the threads on the solenoid become more worn, whereas the switch seems to retain its ease of use.

Eventually, even the best-made parts wear out and valves are no exception. Here, we see older Rain Bird valves to the left, and a newer valve, made by Orbit, to the right. Rain Bird changed its design so that their newer model would no longer fit the footprint of its predecessor. Curiously, the Orbit valve was a direct fit. You can see threaded male/female adapters used on the vertical PVC pipes, which were cut off to allow the placement of the new valve.

TIME TO CHECK YOUR WORK FOR THE REAL WORLD

Ideally, when you are done planning things out, either by using graph paper or PhotoImpact (or something similar), you will be looking at an entire yard's worth of irrigation.

Now it is time to take your work on the page and see how it works in the real world. Grab that graph paper (or print out that file) and head on out to the yard. Make sure your directions are consistent – east is east, south is south, and so on, so that your work on the graph paper is pointing in the same direction as you would want it in your yard.

Does everything on the page STILL make sense? Are those flowerbeds REALLY where you want them, when transposed onto a REAL yard? Are you getting the feeling that the shaded areas may be a challenge for some varieties of plant or grass life? Do you really want your vegetable garden where you put it?

Now would be the time to answer those questions. Go back and re-do your work if your plan doesn't seem to hold up in the real world

Once you have everything where you want it on your graph paper and have checked and rechecked its accuracy, it's time to CONFIRM how you'll route YOUR irrigation to all these locations. Perhaps your layout was similar to the layout presented in the previous examples I used for routing, perhaps not. Regardless, the factors that determine the routing remain the same.

Go to that sketch of your yard and make a mark of some kind where the water source exits the structure of your house. As noted before, there will usually be a hose bib located right here. This is where your manifold (the actual HEART of your irrigation system) will reside. It is at this location that all of your stations (the individual groupings of sprinklers and other irrigation devices) will begin, before reaching out to the more distant points in your yard.

To put this photo into perspective, the sprinklers used have an average range of 6' to 15'. In placing the sprinklers themselves, remember once again that the idea is to make sure that sprinkler A is within such a distance from Sprinkler B that the spray from Sprinkler A doesn't just intersect that of Sprinkler B, but rather easily hits that sprinkler squarely – head to head coverage.

At the square area toward the top of the drawing, this particular yard measures about 23' across. You will notice that there are three separate rows of three sprinklers each in this area. This makes coverage of the area a pretty easy proposition – each sprinkler only needs to reach about 7 ½' – well within the suggested range of the sprinklers.

You will want to calculate in this way, so that a strong wind or additional demands on the water supply (for example, someone showering while the sprinklers are running) doesn't deplete the water pressure to an extent that you end up with dry areas that will eventually turn brown and die.

Now, as we move further down the schematic, you will see that the yard becomes a bit irregular in shape, with a bit more area to cover. The irregular shape in this area makes the usage of simple rows pretty much impossible. To cover this area will take a bit more concentration and creativity. Rather than ponder the actual routing of the irrigation at this point, let's focus instead on just where the sprinklers themselves need to be. For example, you'll always need to make sure that there is coverage at the outer perimeter of your lawn working inwards to the other sprinklers.

Simply placing sprinklers toward the center of the lawn and expecting them to cover the outer reaches of the lawn is not going to work. This mimics what often happens when there is no actual irrigation system in place and the house's occupant instead waters manually via hose.

Now, as we work further, we can now see the irregular portion of the yard is now accounted for. If we were to go back and figure the distance between the sprinkler heads, both side to side and front to back, we would see that in all cases the spacing should pretty easily allow for the spray to hit the adjacent head. We now have the coverage we need. You will see that in this example, two separate stations, and a total of 13 sprinkler heads (6 heads for station #1 and 7 heads for station #2) are providing coverage for this lawn.

Let's move on to the flowerbeds, one bed at a time. In this particular case, the two flowerbeds are actually perpendicular to each other. This means that, as the sun makes its way across the sky, it's going to hit each of these beds differently, resulting in a big variation in the amount of direct sunlight they might receive. So, it makes little sense to put them both on the same station. Just as is the case with trying to combine lawn sprinklers and flowerbed irrigation, to do this would likely result in one flowerbed being irrigated properly with the other overly saturated, or one flowerbed being parched while the other thrives.

So, while the total space occupied by the two flowerbeds would make them pretty easy to cover with just one station, we'll break the coverage into two stations, so that we can more effectively adjust for the specific watering demands of each of them.

Just as was the case with the lawn, each shrub sprinkler made for flowerbeds has a recommended range to it, assuming the water supply going to the sprinkler is optimal. Have a look at the area marked with a "3" (as in Station #3). We can see, by using the proportions on the graph paper, that the flowerbed is roughly two feet wide and about 21' long. Three heads, mounted on risers to give them the clearance they need to get over any foliage that might otherwise block their spray, will provide the coverage needed. Because this flowerbed is relatively narrow, we will need only center-strip patterned sprinkler nozzles. You can see that the three heads located in this area are positioned roughly in the center of the flowerbed, and are evenly spaced, side to side.

Moving on to Area 4, we take the same approach. While this area is going to have different exposure to the sun, and may even contain different types of foliage, the area itself is also fairly narrow, so the same linear approach is used.

Area 5 has a different purpose entirely. There is a vegetable garden situated here, and that will require different equipment. Everything is contained in a fairly small area, so if we were to just use regular shrub sprinklers and risers, we would be wasting water. Also, most vegetables, as well as many plants in general, do better if water is directed at their roots, as opposed to saturating the entire plant.

So, to best suit the needs of this area, we will be going to a drip system – a low pressure system designed for just this purpose. I positioned just one sprinkler riser in this area to service the entire station. You will see, upon closer examination, that the riser is outfitted with a head that allows micro-hoses to be attached to the water coming out here. These micro-hoses, measuring just about ¼ inch in diameter, carry water from the head to the base of the plant.

There are a variety of specially designed parts to maximize the efficiency of this system – the aforementioned head, the micro-hoses, miniature stands to properly position the water flow, and finally, button drippers to direct this flow.

GETTING MORE FAMILIAR WITH THE PARTS YOU WILL BE WORKING WITH

As we move through this process, now would be a good time take a ride down to your local home improvement store and familiarize yourself with these parts. It will help make everything come together for you, conceptually speaking.

Go to the Lawn Section and notice all the different sprinklers, shrub sprinklers, micro sprinklers, specialty parts, etc. that are available. Take a minute or two and read some of the labels to familiarize yourself with what they do, how they are attached, etc.

Then, go to the section where you will find PVC pipe and fittings and do the same thing over there. Notice the products that are available. For piping, you will only want to use Schedule 40 (this refers to the wall thickness and rigidity of the pipe) and (in most cases) ¾ diameter. The fittings will be using make up a pretty big universe. There are couplers (designed to affix two sections of pipe to each other to cover greater length), 90 degree corners, 120 degree corners, T- fittings (both unthreaded - to route a section of pipe perpendicular to an existing pipe, and threaded at the center fitting, which will be ½" in diameter, as opposed to the ends, as this is where the sprinkler riser, shrub riser, etc. will attach.)

This visit will be time well spent. If you spend just 30 minutes doing this, I'm confident you will walk away having a new found confidence that you can, in fact, get this done. I would recommend actually BUYING your parts after you have completed the entire design for your system.

THERE'S A RIGHT AND WRONG WAY TO DIRECT WATER FLOW

If you look at the previous series of graphics, showing the stations being added one on top of the other, take note of the way water is routed to each of them. Each of these areas required some planning as to the best way to direct water from Point A (the water source) to point B (the various sprinklers and irrigation products in a given area). For stations #1 and #2, you can see how the PVC pipes carrying water outward branch off in different direction. This is properly done with the use of the appropriate PVC fittings – elbows, T's, etc. For areas like #3, #4 and #5, this is pretty simple – you are directing water to a specific destination, where it will be redistributed to the sprinklers located in the area that are more or less in a straight line.

In the examples below, we see first the wrong way, and the right way, to direct water flow. In the first illustration, water is merely directed in linear fashion – with some turns, from its start to its finish. Kind of like an amusement park ride, the water follows just one path as it makes its twists and turns before arriving at its final destination.

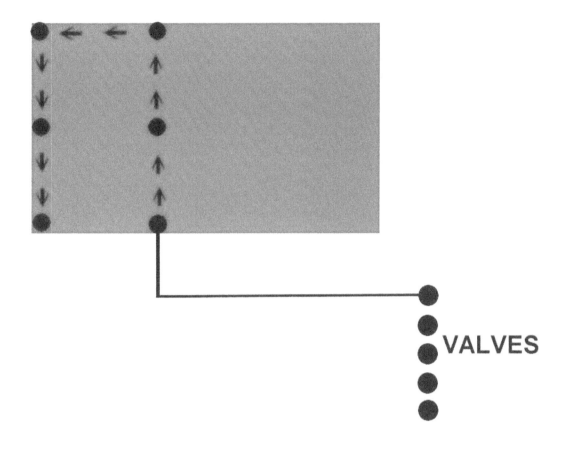

VALVES

A very simple example of water flow being incorrectly routed. In this example, the actual water volume available at the end of the run is going to be appreciably less than at the beginning, and dry spots are likely to result.

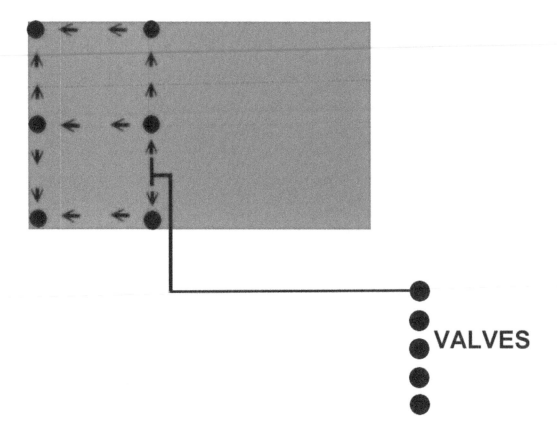

The right way to do it. Now, a more or less equal amount of water will be available among these sprinklers, and much more even water distribution can be achieved.

This will yield inferior results. Water pressure decreases over distance, as each successive sprinkler siphons off pressure. By the time you get to the final sprinkler in the series, water pressure is going to be a fraction of what it was at the start at the first sprinkler. As a result, the effective watering diameter of that last sprinkler is also going to be a fraction of what the first sprinkler could do, likely leaving you with areas that will not get proper coverage and will eventually show dry spots.

Instead, you want to direct water as shown in the second example. Here, water is directed to a single point as it enters the plumbing used to irrigate the entire area, but as it reaches further out, the water flow is redirected EQUALLY to all of the sprinklers at the same time. There will be subtle variations as the water travels over distance, but the water available to each of the sprinkler heads is going to be much more equal from head to head than in the first example. This will allow each of the sprinklers to perform at its best, and yield a watering radius for each that will vary much less, and be much closer to its intended coverage.

Using the above diagrams as a reference, you can now tally up your shopping list (or simply bring it with you if you've enlisted an online service like Rain Bird) and head off to the home improvement store. Be sure and bring your diagrams with you, complete with accurate measurements.

With your design fully conceived (and double-checked, of course), now is the time to purchase the necessary parts and supplies to get started. If your local home improvement store is in close proximity, and you find it less of a chore to approach this build one station at a time, there's certainly nothing wrong with that. In fact, if your vehicle has only limited capacity for what may be as long as 8' lengths of pipe, or you have a big yard that will require a lot of materials, this may even be preferable.

Assuming that you are either using a pre-generated shopping list from a service like Rain Bird's, or have properly calculated how many lengths of pipe and individual fittings you are going to need using the previous station by station graphics as an example, you will also need to account for the parts needed to construct your manifold as well, which again, is the heart of your irrigation system. Make sure you include the parts needed for the manifold on your shopping list, as you will generally want to start the next phase (construction) with your manifold FIRST.

While I have no way of knowing how many individual stations you have chosen to use, if you skip a little ahead to the next chapter (where you will find the subheading 'Assembling the Manifold') before coming back here to stay in order, you will get an idea of what parts are needed to construct your manifold. Besides needing one individual valve (in our case, we are going with anti-siphon valves, as opposed to in-line), you will also need the appropriate fittings – threaded male/slip female adapters, lengths of PVC pipe to connect to your system, elbows, T's, etc.

If you chose to the use the Rain Bird (or similar) service, then at this point you should have these parts already included on your shopping list, so no further inclusion would be necessary.

NOTE: When you shop the aisles of your local home improvement store, you are likely to see both 2 ½" sprinklers and the longer 4" sprinklers on display. Make sure you buy the 4" variety. While there are instances where either size will work, the shorter sprinkler body also comes a shorter "pop – up" height. This means that the height from the top of the sprinkler head to the top of the nozzle when the station is activated is shorter, giving it less clearance over the grass that surrounds it – especially after the grass has grown for a week or so. This will impede the spray, which in turn can lead to dry areas. This won't be an issue with a fresh cut lawn, but regardless of the time of year, your lawn can grow enough in one week to potentially make this an issue.

DIGGING TRENCHES AND BUILDING YOUR SYSTEM

This part is both the most rewarding and most physically challenging of the process. It may help to summarize the steps necessary to complete this portion.

They are:
- *Getting the proper fitting attached to your water source (at the hose bib)*
- *Digging the trenches through which the system plumbing will run and clearing an area for the manifold*
- *Building the manifold (more on this shortly)*
- *Assembling the plumbing together and fitting the sprinklers themselves (station by station)*

Again, though no doubt the most strenuous part of the whole process, the actual building is what I have found to be the most rewarding. It's really a lot of fun to see your vision come together in the real world, and not just on paper.

A repeated word of caution – PACE YOURSELF. Have a realistic expectation of what you can get done in one session and don't exceed it. I've found that, it's better to make your work sessions more about TIME than accomplishing a set amount of work. In other words, don't start by telling yourself "I am going to work non-stop until (insert given part of project is finished". Rather, tell yourself "Today I will devote (insert given number of minutes or hours) to this project"

The reason is fairly simple - things don't always go exactly as planned. You may have forgotten a part at the store, or purchased the wrong part. You may get interrupted at a certain point. You may feel the need to go back and have a second look at your plans, etc.

If you parcel out your sessions in terms of time, you will find all of these unforeseen circumstances less intrusive to the rest of your time/life. You may not get quite as much accomplished on a given day, but you also will not feel that sense of discouragement that comes with looking at the clock and realizing that you were toiling a lot longer than you had planned, and have neglected other things you needed to get done that day.

For most of us, installing a sprinkler system is a 'weekend warrior' type of project – as our every day jobs do not permit us the time to get much done during the work week. But there are likely other demands on your time away from work. Parceling out your work in time blocks allows you to make sure these other demands are not neglected, and that you don't begin to resent what you've embarked upon because of it.

In order to make these sessions more productive, try your best to organize just what you need handy to get the job done. As you reach your work site, make sure every tool, part, and accessory you are going to need for this step is within reach. You can really save a lot of time by not having to run back and forth to the garage.

GETTING THE PROPER FITTING ATTACHED TO YOUR WATER SUPPLY

This is a step where I ***strongly*** recommend enlisting the services of a professional plumber. You are going to need to tie in to your existing water supply (again, generally located near where your hose bib is) with a fitting that will allow you to siphon off water used by your irrigation system. You are not attaching directly to the bib itself, but rather to water supply that feeds it.

As you can see in photo below, the t-fitting is professionally attached to the existing plumbing and is of sufficient length so that you can attach a separate shut off valve solely for the sprinkler system itself. This way, if you ever need to do any work on the system itself (and you will, because parts wear out, things need to be adjusted over time, etc.) you can shut off the water supply to the sprinkler system without having to shut off the water supply to the house. You can still take a shower, do dishes, etc. while you are working on the sprinkler system with the water off. (Just a note – you can't work on the system with the water on, because the water pressure would cause water to simply run through what you are attaching, making a mess, as well as making your work impossible.

If you happen to be a plumber, or if you have confidence in your pipe brazing skills, then go ahead and do this step yourself as well. Few people have the requisite skill for this part, and the potential results of doing this wrong are too expensive to reconcile taking a chance on it. Most plumbers will charge in the area of $100-$200 to attach this fitting and, to me anyway, the price is well worth making sure this part is done right.

Again, to reiterate, unless you have professional level pipe brazing skills, it may be worth it to have a licensed plumber install the T fitting that will connect the manifold to the house water supply.

DIGGING THE TRENCHES

PLEASE NOTE, ABOVE ALL ELSE: Regardless of whether you decide to dig your ditches with a pick axe and shovel, or with an automated trencher, **ALWAYS, ALWAYS** call your local utility company to find out where your underground lines are located. Do not skip this step. In some areas, natural gas pipes can be surprisingly close to ground level, and may be placed right smack in the middle of a plot of land. You **DO NOT WANT** to strike these pipes with your pick, a trencher, or any other object. At the very least, you will have a costly repair to have to worry about. Serious injury or worse can result from striking a gas line with sufficient force. In areas where electricity also runs underground, this goes double.

With your design close by to refer to, now you will set about digging the trenches that will house the plumbing for your system – the PVC pipes and fittings that carry the water from the source to where you need it. A little bit of planning and analysis can save some work here. For example, can you house more than one PVC line in a trench? No reason why not, as long as the trench is dug out sufficiently wide. In fact, many effective layouts will result in multiple lines running through trenches at least part of the way. It saves time, and provided the lines are not crammed on top of each other (which can result in eventual breakage) there is no downside.

It's a good idea to dig your trenches FROM the water source out to your sprinklers. With the design checked and double checked after having being committed to paper, I'd recommend mapping out this very design, using stakes/flags and string (POLICE TAPE SHOULD BE USED AROUND THE PERIMETER AND ANYWHERE ELSE WHERE TRIPPING WOULD BE A CONCERN), on your actual lawn.

Just to reiterate, those proper locations should be determined by mapping out the individual sprinkler locations comprising each section. As you begin this step, it is ALWAYS a good idea to recheck your work by taking a measuring tape to your freshly placed flags. You will want to make sure that a) they are properly situated in the 'real world' and b) none of the distances between any two on the same station exceed the recommended range of the individual sprinklers being used. In fact, it's a good idea to be somewhat UNDER this maximum range.

I would also recommend taking some pictures of your work as the trenching begins and as you progress. The pictures will provide you with a sort of BLUEPRINT of your work.

Over time, you may forget just where you put those trenches and what pipe leads where, because when this project is finished, only the sprinkler heads themselves will be visible, and you will not necessarily remember the direction of the PVC pipes that connect them. If you have a visual record of what you have done, it makes things a world easier should there ever be problems down the line – a broken line (especially common if your system is adjacent to a driveway).

You will also need to decide just HOW you plan on digging your trenches. Will you be doing so MANUALLY, using a pick axe and a shovel, or will you use a trencher, commonly available at home improvement rental departments, as well as companies that rent heavy equipment - Hertz, (hertzequip.com) for example?

The automated route definitely saves physical effort, as well as time. With the ground adequately prepared by going through the rototilling process already described, and once again, **WITH ALL UNDERGROUND UTILITY LINES PROPERLY ACCOUNTED FOR**, you can cut trenches surprisingly easily with a trencher, and the equipment is not that hard to use. Need wider trenches? Simply make multiple passes.

The "walk behind" variety of trencher, the most applicable kind for more residential applications, will make a trench about 3"- 4" wide, and is pretty easy to control. These machines generally run on gasoline, not unlike a lawn mower. An adjustable swivel determines just how deep the cutting goes, with depths of up to 2' feet (more than you would ever need in most cases) easily attainable.

However, even fairly involved systems are more often than not trenched by hand, with a shovel. If you decide to go this route, then just remember to pace yourself, and keep your trenches accurate and straight by continually checking your work along the way.

So, as you start digging your trenches, just how deep and how wide should they be? Well, as far as depth, you want all your PVC pipes to be far enough down from the surface that they cannot be easily affected by foot traffic, lawnmowers, the ground settling (settling is more pronounced at surface level than it is further down). Also, you need to make sure that there will be enough depth to accommodate a 90 degree fitting that connect your sprinklers, via risers, to your PVC piping, some additional length for the riser itself, and the body of the sprinkler, which is about five inches in height. I generally dig my trenches at about ten to twelve inches of depth.

As far as the width of the trenches – THAT will be determined by the number of PVC pipes running through it. With just one pipe to have to worry about and assuming you have decided to dig your trenches manually, as I generally do, a common trenching shovel can be used. You can get one at any home improvement store for about $30. A trenching shovel is narrower than its more commonly used counterpart – generally about five inches wide. The net effect of this, besides digging a narrower trench, is that you will actually only be moving the amount of dirt necessary to run the pipe, meaning that no effort will be wasted moving dirt around that could have stayed in place.

On the other hand, if you are planning things out in such a way that a few pipes may be running a certain amount of length while parallel, perhaps before turning off in separate directions, a common shovel may be more useful. Your trenches really won't require much width beyond what is literally needed to for the pipe to sit side by side (and not on top of each other), but it is good to have a couple of inches on either side to work with as you are attaching pieces together. After you've begun to dig, you will soon get a feel for what you are doing.

You will want to pay close attention to is the relative CONSISTENCY of the depth of your trenches, you don't want to have your trenches to have too much variation as you move forward. PVC pipes have the ability to bend somewhat, but to go from depths (for example) 8" to 16"" back to 8", especially in a short section will put stress on the pipe from bending under any substantial weight may lead to leaks or breakage down the line. Also, if you take precautions to make sure your trenches are relatively level along their entire length, it will make getting your sprinkler bodies and risers nice and perpendicular to the ground a lot easier a little later.

Think about it. If your pipe is at an angle, and yet the fixture holding your sprinkler is fixed at a 90-degree angle (in other words, perpendicular to the ground) then the end result cannot help but be flawed, with the top of the sprinkler leaning backwards or forwards toward the pipe it is connected to.

So, how do you take precautions to get your trenches nice and level? There are actually a couple of things you can do. For starters you can just take a yardstick, preferably a metal one or one that you don't mind getting soiled, and take periodic measurements along the way by measuring perpendicular to the bottom of the trench. If the land at ground level is nice and flat, or very close to it, this should keep everything going along in a pretty consistent manner.

You can also use a level for this. Periodically place the level in a cleanly dug trench and see how you are doing. You don't need ABSOLUTE precision here, but you don't want huge variations in the depth of the trench that may either bend the pipe under weight of the dirt, or angle your sprinklers in such a way as to compromise their effectiveness (and make them look a little unprofessional, as well).

How many pipes can sit side by side in a trench? As many as you need, really. Although the more you do decide to place in a given trench, the more precise you need to be with your cutting and measurements to make sure the pipes don't end up on top of each other as they are making turns. Properly and efficiently combining PVC pipes into the same trench will save you an appreciable amount of labor as you move forward. If in doubt, you can go back and refer to the series of graphics showing each individual station being designed. This will also give you an idea as to where you can combine locations of PVC pipe.

The photo just below shows several pipes running from the sprinkler manifold to the first turn. You will see that the trench that is housing these pipes is pretty wide (it would have to be to keep them from being stacked on top of each other) and that the pipes are fairly evenly spaced apart from each other. As they make their turn, the variations in their lengths, with the longer pipe being furthest from the bend, and the shortest pipe being at the bend, maintain their position relative to each other.

As you can see here, a trench wide enough to accommodate several PVC pipes side by side has been created out from the manifold. There has also been sufficient dirt removed from under the manifold to allow it to sit level while the PVC pipes are run out to their various locations.

CREATING SPACE FOR THE MANIFOLD

Properly placing your manifold will require you to clear out dirt at the area where you are connecting it to your water supply. It is from here that the individual trenches will originate, before fanning out to the various locations in your yard.

Depending on how many valves you've decided upon, you will likely need to clear out around 2 ½' at the point where the manifold will be situated. Just to recap, as far as depth, I would recommend you going with about 10-12 inches below the existing level of the ground at that point. This way, the pipes that extend outward from the manifold will sit relatively flat in their ditches, which makes everything else fit better.

If your schematic has been planned out correctly, it's likely that your widest trench will be situated just in front of the manifold, as the various PVC pipes mounted underneath their respective valves will likely be pointed straight ahead (at least for most of them) for at least a little bit of distance before making their respective turns.

Now that it is time to put shovel to dirt, you should have a clear understanding of what lies ahead. If not, go back and see what it is that is tripping you up. No one likes to waste time or brain power if something has to be redone, but it's even more frustrating to waste MANUAL LABOR in the same manner. No reason to make this part of the process overly complicated, as from here it is essentially just trenching from point A to point B, etc., but the key here is to make sure your respective 'points' are where they should be. If a re-do of some kind is needed, at least it is unlikely that any serious consequences, save for physical effort, have resulted.

So, on with the grunt work. As noted before, I think it is best to start digging at the point of the water source OUT to where your plumbing lines are going.

Now, at this point you will have long since worked on the soil with a tiller and soil additives so that it is no longer compacted, but wetting down the soil an hour or so before working on will soften the dirt and helps maintain more consistent trenches as you dig.

As you dig in around that area where the 'T' fitting that will send water to your system is located, again you'll need to account for the width of your manifold, and then some. This way, when you are ready to place the manifold, you will have some working room around it, which will make it easier to get it nice and level.

Obviously, the more valves you will be using, the more width you are going to need.

You don't want to bunch the valves too close together, so as to minimize their foot print. Sprinkler valves are not particularly attractive, so there is a tendency to want them to take up as little area as possible. Perfectly understandable. But there is a counterpoint here.

One day, even the most dependable of valves will break, or at least need some work. Also, you may need to manually adjust the output of your valves, which (on some models) is done by turning the SOLENOID (the black cylindrical knob on the back half of the valve). And when either of these happens, you will want at least SOME clearance between the valves. Somewhere around the width of a fist, maybe. I generally situate mine 4" from each other, on center. This means that, prior to the actual valves that sit atop the manifold being connected, the center point of one VERTICAL PVC PIPE connected to that valve with be 4" from the one next to it, using the very center of the pipe as a reference point.

The depth of the trench at the manifold should be somewhere in the neighborhood of the trenches dug elsewhere in the yard – 10-12 inches or so. Again, you don 't want a huge amount of variation in the depth of your trenches, as it can put a bend on the lines when the area is backfilled with dirt, and it can cause the sprinklers at the end of the trench to settle at an angle. So try to keep that depth fairly consistent.

As your trenches extend outward from the area where the manifold will be, you should have them all marked by now - preferably with flags (readily available at home improvement stores) and some police tape. You will want to do this for all of your trenches, as it will keep your work focused, and keep your trenches fairly straight. Just remember which side of the trench the flags and tape are to be situated on. In other words, if you start digging with the tape to the left of your shovel as you move forward, make sure you keep it that way. Otherwise, an unplanned veer or turn could mean a do-over.

As a precaution, I would also recommend buying some caution tape, and marking the entire perimeter area off where possible. You don't want door to door salesmen, the postman, or anyone else taking a tumble on your property.

If you find the ground difficult to work with, and you have chosen to dig your ditches manually (with a pick and shovel) you may want to loosen it up a bit with a pick. And, I can't emphasize enough at this point - always keep a realistic perspective on how much you can get accomplished at one time. Noted previously, I think it's a better idea to plan out a day's work in TIME increments (i.e. "I will work at this for 30 minutes today"), as opposed to sheer progress ("I am going to dig 20 feet of trenches today") The latter may seem more appealing in that it would seem to prompt you to get more done, it can also sour you on the project by causing you to over-exert to make your 'deadline'.

There's likely not much of a ticking clock on your project, save for the one you have perhaps set yourself, so don't wear yourself out before you've even made much headway.

Periodically, as you make progress, you may want to take a step back and make sure your PROGRESS is what you intended – meaning that you are sticking with the plan you formulated. If there are trenches that will meet at a certain point on the yard, is that junction going to end up where you intended? If your trenches are supposed to be running parallel to each other in certain areas, are they coming out a uniform distance as you progress along the length of the ditch? It's easy to lose perspective as you gain focus. You may be concentrating so hard on making sure you are progressing forward with those trenches that you may not even notice that you veered off parallel in the process. When in doubt, grab a measuring tape and check. Way better to make a correction on 4' of ditch than 20'.

Carefully checking the placement of those flags and the tape should be pretty much all that is needed with this. But in addition, pace yourself, taking some time here and there to step back and check your work.

A SPECIAL CIRCUMSTANCE: TUNNELING UNDER SIDEWALK AND OTHER OBSTACLES

There are certain situations where you might find yourself wanting to bring your ditches underneath an obstacle – perhaps a stretch of sidewalk, another surface obstacle. This can be done a couple of ways

The best way would be to go to your local home improvement store and purchase the PVC part specially made for this purpose. I know that Orbit makes a specific kit, as likely do a couple of other manufactures. Literally speaking, the kit will consist of a conical fitting to be primed and attached with PVC cement to the end of a length of PVC pipe that will need to be about as long as the width of sidewalk you are tunneling under. Additionally, there should be another fitting that is threaded internally to fit a common garden hose. This piece will be attached to the other end of the length of PVC pipe. The increasing pressure caused by constricting the flow of water results in a more powerful stream – much like what happens when you put your thumb or finger over the hose to create a stronger jet while washing a car or cleaning your driveway. This stream – though very small in diameter, will be effective in clearing a pathway underneath an obstacle or stretch of sidewalk. It should only take about a minute to get where you are going. You'll need to dig out a ditch at least as deep as the thickness of the sidewalk you are working with so that you can get the length of PVC pipe level as you work your way underneath it.

Here's a pretty good video showing the process.

https://www.youtube.com/watch?v=3Kv9x8bAWVM

Just one more word of caution . . . . When performing this step, take extra care to make sure you are pointing that pressurized stream exactly in the direction you want it. While it's true that you can always go back and redirect the excavation, it is extra work, and if you clear too much space under any cement, you make it more prone to cracking later on.

FINISHING UP THIS PART OF THE PROCESS

After carefully digging the pathway each of your sprinkler stations will take, so that the trenches terminate at their destination, be sure to also go back and trace the pathway of each station from valve to the final sprinkler head on each station. Any given sprinkler head should end about 2" away from any sidewalk, driveway, etc. to reduce its chance of being driven over, stepped on, etc. You'll find that it is impossible to avoid some damage to your sprinkler heads over time – the most common culprit being lawn mower damage - but if you avoid placing the sprinkler right at the edge of the sidewalk or driveway, it will definitely give you a head start in avoiding having to replace parts any more often than necessary.

You'll want to use police tape (or twine) to mark out your measurements and provide a directional guide BEFORE you begin digging any trenches. When properly measured out, this will keep everything nice and linear. You should also use police tape around the perimeter of any area where you want to keep foot traffic away, or could pose a potential tripping danger. Think postal service in the case of a front lawn. For the perimeter, always use police/caution tape, as you want this warning to be as visible as possible.

ASSEMBLING THE MANIFOLD

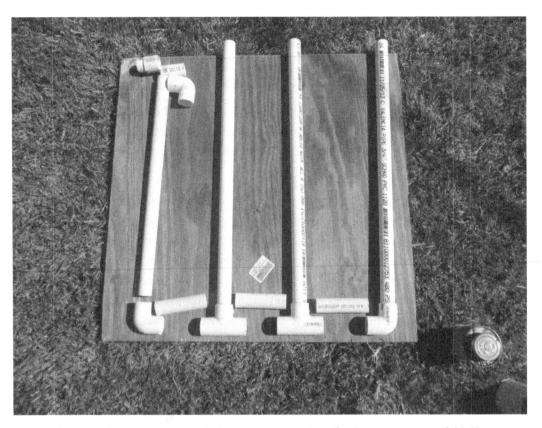

Shown here are the parts necessary to build the rear portion of a three station manifold. The parts themselves are laid out on the same plywood board that will remain in place during the assembly process, as explained later. The PVC pipe on the left may not necessarily end up parallel to the three vertical pipes that will each hold valves, since the manifold may need to sit further out from the house than the current position of the water source, as shown immediately below.

Looking directly down from above the manifold, you can see that the PVC pipe on the right is not completely parallel to the front of the house, but rather is on a slight angle forward from top to bottom. This allows more working space on the manifold should any future work need to be done on the valves, which almost certainly will happen.

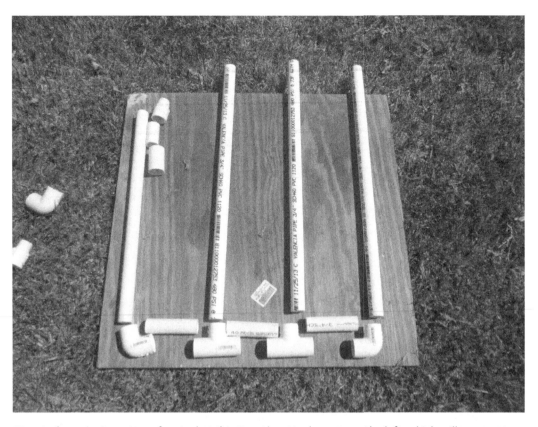

Here is the same inventory of parts, but this time the attachments on the left, which will connect to a water source, are laid out for a vertical insertion, as shown in the photo below. Obviously, the final position of the manifold, and therefore its construction, will be determined by whether or not you have had the T-fitting installed pointing left or right. In this case, the T-fitting would have been installed pointing to the right.

The first two photos show the PVC parts used to build the manifold spread out on a level plywood board. If you look to the left of each, you will see a slight variation. One version will handle a more horizontally oriented insertion, while the second a vertical. The threaded male adapter used to tie the manifold into the shut off valve and water supply for the vertical example is shown in the foreground, properly treated with Teflon tape.

Now that the trenches are dug, and have all been checked to determine that they are just where you want them, it's time to start building your manifold, which again, is akin to the "heart" of your system. Its valves open and close to regulate the flow of water to the 'circulatory system" – that series of PVC pipes, elbows and T's that make up the plumbing. Because the manifold is such an essential part of any sprinkler system, its assembly may seem a little daunting, but it really isn't difficult at all.

You may want to take a minute or two and get clear on just what the manifold does, as this will help you gain a bit of confidence in putting it together correctly. For starters, that T fitting that you had the plumber install (or perhaps YOU installed) will send water to your system when the valve installed specifically for the system is set to the "open" position. If you recall, this valve is there to allow you to shut water off to your sprinkler system without having to stop the water flow to the rest of the house.

Once water enters the manifold through the "T" fitting, it is sent downward to the bottom PVC pipe that runs parallel to the ground. Once the water fills this pipe, its continued flow will cause the vertical PVC pipes to fill with water. Once they are filled, pressure builds, and the water will naturally flow to the OPEN valve – the valve whose station has been "ordered" by the timer to open and let the water flow out.

What causes the valve to open? The process begins with the SOLENOID on the valve – that cylindrical part at the top of the rear part of the valve with the electrical wires attached. The solenoid controls the opening and closing of the seal in the rear of the valve, determining whether or not water can get through to the front.

Regardless of whether the solenoid is opened manually (by twisting open the solenoid to let water flow or on Orbit valves, by turning a switch) or electrically (when electrical current flowing to the valve ALSO causes it to open) , the water flow then moves up one of the rear vertical pipes that comprise the manifold, past the rear part of the valve, down the actuator (the relatively flat, front part of the valve), down the front vertical pipe, where it flows out through the PVC plumbing you have (or will have) installed.

Now, you may ask "What would happen if ALL the valves were closed?"

Well . . . nothing.

No different than how faucets work in the other parts of your house. Like those faucets, the valves are actually electric "gatekeepers", controlling whether or not, as well as how powerfully, water comes out of the valve and into the system.

When installing the manifold, you may also be tempted to try and keep it sitting as low as possible, by using shorter vertical pipes on the front and back to make it less obvious when sitting in place. Not a bad idea in theory, but it's generally recommended by most manufacturer that the valve be at least six inches ABOVE the highest sprinkler head on the station that valve controls.

The reason? Gravity. See, if that valve is lower, or at the same level, as that sprinkler, then water can continue to seep out of the head of the sprinkler, even when it is no longer supposed to be running, because there will be no gravitational force to clear the excess water in the line. I usually figure on my valves being about a foot above the ground where they are situated. Admittedly somewhat less than decorative, your manifold can always be covered with a decorative box (readily available at the home improvement store).

While we are on the subject of valves, you may also wonder what the term "anti-siphon" even means. You will see this term applied to the vast majority of above ground valves. It's actually a pretty simple concept. "Anti-siphon" merely means the valves will only allow water to flow one way, and no matter what happens with the water pressure, the flow will not reverse itself and send water, mixed with dirt and perhaps a few small pebbles and grass shavings, back into your water system for drinking.

So, once you have determined the height of the valves (combining the depth below ground with the elevation above ground to come up with the correct length to which to cut the PVC pipes), make a note of your calculations, so that you cut the PVC evenly and each of your valves ends up at the same height when you are finished.

The accompanying photos show the process of assembling a manifold from beginning (assembling the back of the manifold as it attaches to your exterior plumbing) to the end (leaving off where the underground PVC pipes in their trenches will carry water to the predetermined sprinkler locations on your lawn.

I'm pretty sure you will be able to follow along with the photos, but just in case something does momentarily trip you up, go back over to the parts of the process immediately before it, and I still think things will become clear.

VERY IMPORTANT . . . . DON'T forget is to use Teflon tape on ALL of the threaded male fittings, save for the sprinklers and their risers. This is an essential step, as the Teflon forms a tight seal that keeps water, even water under pressure, from leaking out, as would otherwise happen without the Teflon tape.

You will see this part of the process as well in the accompanying photos.

With the exception of where your sprinklers attach to the risers (there is not nearly as much pressure coming through at this point and none when the valve controlling it closed), a good rule of thumb is to wrap any visible threads you see with Teflon tape upon installation – the adapters coming out of the valves, the fixture that attaches your manifold to a water source, anytime you decide to convert a sprinkler riser to a drip or pressure system – etc., etc. There is no downside and the minimal extra effort is minimal in achieving a nice, watertight seal.

Now that you know a little more about what the manifold does, and what the individual parts that comprise the manifold do, it's time to put it together.

I prefer to assemble the rear portion of the manifold, creating one piece that is then moved into place where dirt has been excavated adjacent to the water supply and then connected to the water supply by adding a PVC fitting that will connect to the "T" that has been installed. (Definitely do not forget the Teflon tape with this step – it WILL result in water leakage as the water pressure builds between the "T" and the entrance to the manifold.

BUILDING THE MANIFOLD – STEP BY STEP

The individual steps described are backed up with some pictures, so if there is any uncertainty as you move forward, just have a look at the accompanying picture and it should clear things up for you. The photos used illustrate the steps to be taken for a three station (and therefore, three valve) system, but the procedure would be exactly the same for a six station system, just with the addition of more PVC pipe, and of course, more valves connected to the pipes.

Cut the bottom PVC pipe sections

These are going to be the pieces that will, in turn, be fitted into PVC 'T's and elbows, etc. from which the vertical pipes extend upward. Before you make the first cut, be certain that you have determined how far apart you are going to have your valves situated, as these pieces are part of what determines that final distance. In determining this distance, make sure you are using a uniform system of measurement. For example, determine in advance that you are going to measure this distance ON CENTER from solenoid to solenoid (the black knob that sits atop the valve), actuator to actuator (the cylindrical portion situated at the front of the valve), or whatever you choose. ON CENTER, of course meaning, "from the center of one, to the center of the next one".

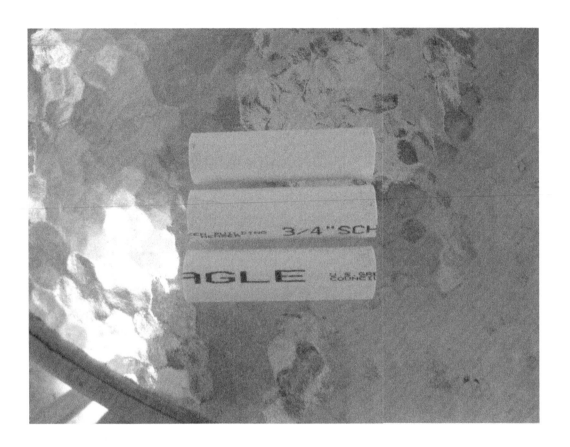

Three horizontal sections that will be used to connect the vertical PVC pieces
are cut to size, and then checked for uniformity.

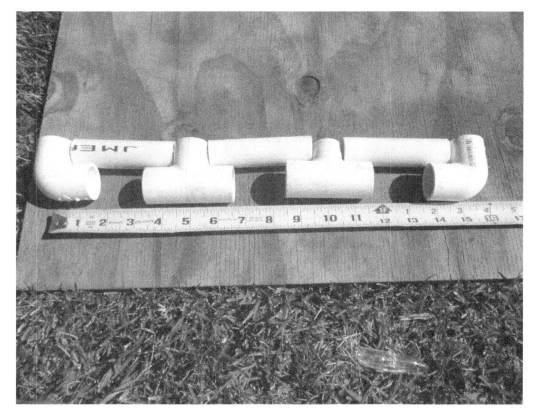

Once the pieces are laid out in the context of the other parts being used, it gives you a better idea as to how these measurements were arrived at. If you look closely, the approximate midway point of each T and the elbow to the right are right about five inches apart, as planned.

So, if you have determined, for example, that the valves are to be five inches apart ON CENTER, you can cut your pieces to about 3 3/4". Why the difference? Because the PVC pipe, as it is inserted into the "T" fitting, actually stops because of a détente (intentional protrusion) in the T that is located just before the single perpendicular hole of the "T" and of course, not at its halfway point (because it would block the flow of water through the piece).

If you want to do a sort of mockup, that is probably the best approach, but be careful that the pieces are totally clean, and free of any dirt or grime. It takes very little to create a semi-permanent seal inside the PVC pieces that WILL make pulling them apart very challenging.

Cut out the vertical pipes for the rear part of the manifold.

These are the sections that run from the back of the valve down to below ground level. Their height, as noted before, will be determined by just how far below ground your ditches have been dug, added to how high your valves will be above ground. So, if your ditches are 10" inches below the surface, and you want your valves to be 12" inches ABOVE surface, you will want to cut these sections at 22"

Before any PVC cement is applied, each interior has to be thoroughly treated with PVC primer, the purple substance shown here. Yes, it does stain, so if you are not planning on covering the manifold after completion, you will want to be very careful when applying primer. The interior of both parts being fitted should receive primer.

Here we see PVC cement being applied to the primed area. The same thing will be done to the interior of the fitting on which it is placed. It takes only a few seconds for PVC primer to dry, and it should be totally dry before the cement is applied, as shown.

Connect the vertical pipes to PVC "T's" and elbow

At the bottom end of each of these pieces, you will be connecting, through the use of PVC primer and then PVC cement, the PVC "T's" and elbows. You won't be using the "T's" on the last of the pipes (the one furthest from the water source). On this section vertical pipe sections on both ends you will instead be using PVC elbows. Once you are finished with this step, you should end up with a series of 22" PVC pipes that have either T's or elbows attached to them at the bottom. Have another look at the accompanying photo if you are unclear on this.

If you look to the PVC pipe on the right, you will see the bottom fitting (an elbow) properly attached.

The second fitting is attached in the same manner.

. . . . . And the third. The PVC pipe that will run vertically (not shown here) will require its bottom fitting to be attached in the same manner.

Using the 3 ¼" sections you cut during Step 1, connect these pieces.

There is a reason for doing things in THIS exact sequence, as opposed to improvising and skipping steps.

After you have attached an elbow to the bottom of the PVC pipe that will be connected to the first pipe in the sequence, and then have connected the first bottom PVC section into one end of that elbow, you can use any completely flat area to help you get those sections even with each other. While you can always "eyeball" your way through these steps, you will likely not get everything lined up this way. The valves will work as long as you get them close to vertical, the manifold will end up looking uneven.

So instead, you can take that first piece of vertical pipe with an elbow attached to the bottom, connect the first bottom PVC section that runs BETWEEN the valves, and lay the whole thing down on the ground (provided the ground is level – if not use a plywood board or something similar, as shown in the accompanying photos). At this point, the elbow will be lying on its side, and the PVC pipe that sticks out of it will also be resting on the floor.

You can then take the next vertical pipe/T connection and attach it to the bottom PVC section sticking out of the elbow, by holding the first section against the ground (or plywood), inserting the vertical pipe piece (after of course, priming it and applying PVC cement) so that it is NOT resting on the ground, but rather is maybe a foot off the ground, and the rotating the new piece downward until it too is resting on the floor.

This way, you'll end up with vertical pipes that appear more even when upright and the act of inserting the vertical pipe into the fittings this way does a good job of evenly distributing the PVC cement, resulting in a tight seal.

Make sure you don't try to move the parts around for at least a couple of minutes or so after doing this. While the pieces are likely to have set after just a few seconds, if the glue is even just a little short of setting and the pieces become dislodged it will have an effect on the final seal.

Keep this up for the sections in the MIDDLE of the manifold. The pipes leading to both the first and the last vertical pipe in the manifold will have elbows attached, instead of T's, as these portions need to be closed, meaning the water flow can't be allowed to escape out of the manifold, but rather is directed to the next station in the manifold.

Once you are through with this process, you should end up with the vertical pipes that make up the rear portion of the manifold all attached in a row, like this . . .

The rear portion of the manifold is now completely assembled.

Attach this rear portion of the manifold to your water supply, by using a threaded male adapter, with the slip end facing the manifold.

This is another application where it is ESSENTIAL that you use Teflon tape. Where the T was installed to redirect water to your sprinkler system, you will want to carefully cover the threaded area of a male threaded/slip adapter with Teflon tape, then insert this threaded portion into the threaded portion of the T and rotate it clockwise until it is very snug.

Before bonding everything together you will want to do a test fitting. Take the rear portion of the manifold you have created, and set it down on the ground in the excavated area you have dug out near your water source, and make sure it can sit in a position perpendicular to the ground line. You can use a common level to check its position for both vertical and horizontal level.

Once it's in the position you want it, you can then cut the portion of PVC that will extend from the male threaded/slip adapter to the inlet on this portion of the manifold (where the water supply enters). In measuring the section of PVC pipe that will make this run, be sure and allow for the extra depth needed to make a secure joint between the pipe and the first elbow that leads downwards, as shown.

With this section in place and secured properly to the water supply, the rear portion of the manifold should be completed and look something like this:

In this photo, we can clearly see the "T" fitting attached to the water source at the right. The colored knob at lower right is the shutoff valve for the entire valve. Further up, and to the left, you can see another valve that controls water flow to the manifold itself. This allows you to shut off water to the sprinkler system without doing the same to the house itself.

Now, you will want to secure it in place by backfilling any dirt needed underneath it so that it sits level on the ground and is not simply hanging from where it is connected. Be very careful not to get any dirt down the vertical piping. Double check to make sure, once the manifold is sitting on the backfilled and compressed dirt, that it sits level, both side to side and from back to front.

INSTALLING THE VALVES

Here are the three anti-siphon valves, sitting ready for use. Immediately below each of them is a threaded male adapter that will be prepared with Teflon tape over its threads before being attached to each valve. The valves will then be positioned on the vertical pipes with the use of PVC primer and cement. Each will be prepared the same way as before – primer first then cement and finally, the attachment of the valve by placing it onto the vertical pipe and then rotating around into position to get the alignment correct and the cement properly distributed.

The rear portion of the manifold is completely assembled, and one valve has been attached. Again, always make sure to use Teflon tape over the threads of the male adapter that will sit inside the valve.

Two valves on.

. . . .and all three. Again, you can just as easily position the rear portion of the manifold in place and then attach the valves. It's a matter of preference.

With the rear portion of the manifold in place and secure, now it is time to start installing the valves that go on top of the vertical pipes. For the purposes of this project, we are going to assume that we will be installing anti-siphon, above-ground valves (as opposed to in-line valves).

Because this is a part of the system that will have to endure a substantial amount of water pressure, make sure the connection is secure, but you don't need to overdo it. If you exert too much force, it is possible to strip the threads on the valve openings.

Once the adapter is securely fastened to the valve *(and after making sure you have lined the threads of the adapter with Teflon tape)*, you can double check that the connection is as tight as practical. After doing so, you can then take the valve, with the adapters attached to the rear portion of the valve (the one underneath the solenoid) and position over the vertical pipe you intend to connect it to.

Treat both the inside of the adapter (the 'slip') portion, and the end of the vertical pipe it is to be attached to first with PVC primer, and then evenly spread PVC cement, also on both ends. If the PVC cement truly is applied evenly and correctly, the two surfaces to be connected are likely going to be well covered in PVC cement, but it is still a good practice to be able to make at least a 1/4 to 1/2 turn with the valve, once installed, to better spread the cement around. Use only enough glue to cover the surfaces being bonded and no more. If over-applied the excess will tend to run downward and discolor the otherwise white PVC pipe – though you can always paint the manifold if you are a stickler for tidiness.

Just a reminder/caution – ***PVC cement dries very quickly***!! As you pivot that valve around on the vertical PVC pipe, it's important to ***a) stand/sit in front of the connection so that you can get a better vantage point to determine if the valve is pointing straight ahead and b) get the valve to that position as quickly as possible***. Just as with previous steps, as long as you are in the ballpark as far as the valves being straight is concerned, everything should work fine, but again, you want this work to look as good as possible when you are finished, so extra steps like double-checking the straightness of the valves is a good way to go.

Once the first valve is where you want it, with the PVC cement properly set to keep it that way, it is easier to get the others to follow suit. Stay in front of the manifold, so that you can keep checking the uniformity of the valve position and get the valve to where it needs to be quickly, before the cement dries.

Again, when you are putting your stations together this way, make sure you are using Teflon tape anywhere you see exposed threads. This will help keep pressure related leaks from occurring.

THE FRONT PORTION OF THE MANIFOLD

Up to this point, if everything has gone correctly, you should now be left with the rear portion of the manifold sitting in place and connected to your water source at the side with an anti-siphon valve sitting atop each rear vertical pipe of the manifold.

With all of the valves now assembled and properly positioned, the manifold just awaits connection to the water supply and the assembly of the downward PVC pipes leading out to the lawn. The installation of the valves can just as easily be done with the rear portion of the manifold already connected to the water supply.

You can now begin the installation of the vertical pipe leading downward, past ground surface level, where your trench has been excavated for the front of the manifold. The plumbing that will be contained in your trenches leads out from this vertical piping to the horizontal piping that powers the individual sprinklers that terminate the system.

So, to complete the manifold, it's now just a matter of bringing those front vertical pipes down to the right level (low enough so that the PVC pipes that will run perpendicular to them will rest on the floor of each of the ditches you have created, but high enough so that there is room to connect the horizontal pipes).

You will want to cut each of these vertical pipes accordingly, and there should be enough ground excavated underneath them (a few inches) so that you can attach the necessary fittings that lead outward to your sprinklers. While the next step after this will be to connect PVC elbows at the bottom to create that perpendicular joint between these pipes and the pipes that run the ditches, don't do so just yet. I'll explain . . .

Just as when you began to create the rear portion of the manifold, you placed the assembly down against the ground to give you a sort of visual reference point to help create straight parallel connections, you can use a similar method at this stage to do the same – making sure that the first sections of the pipes that connect out from the front vertical pipes stay relatively parallel to each other and (or worse) don't overlap before they make their respective turns out to the various positions in your yard.

So, instead of connecting the elbows onto the bottoms of the front vertical pipes, first connect a length of PVC pipe to the elbows themselves, using the same method of first preparing the pipe with PVC primer, then using the PVC cement to forge this bond. Then, begin with either the outer- most or innermost vertical pipe, connect the elbow onto the pipe that runs down vertically from the front of the valve, rotating the horizontal portion you just attached enough to spread the PVC cement evenly, and then quickly (before the cement dries) positioning the horizontal pipe as parallel to the side of the ditch as you can. This will give you a good starting reference point for the other connections to come afterward.

This photo shows the horizontal plumbing out to the lawn beginning to take shape. Note that in this particular case, some of the PVC piping will be routed UNDER existing plumbing. This area is also more thoroughly excavated because eventually concrete will be added to complete a patio not visible in this photo.

With this first horizontal pipe (PVC elbow and a length of PVC pipe) now in place and parallel relative to the ditch, you can now do the same with the other piping to be connected, working your way from this first connection to the other side without skipping any of the valves. This will make creating parallel runs much easier.

There are certain situations where the PVC pipes running from the front of the valves will make an immediate turn right at the connection, but more often than not, at least a few of the stations you have created will share some common ground before going their respective ways.

THE SYSTEM BEGINS TO TAKE SHAPE

Make sure you have that schematic you created previously close by and handy to refer to. You should have also marked the position of each sprinkler with a flag or other easily recognizable object that can be staked into the ground, taking care never to exceed the maximum recommended range of any of the sprinklers being used. I find that it is easiest to work on a single station at a time once the area where the stations share a common run is finished.

Here is an open trench, with PVC pipe and sprinkler risers clearly visible. As you can see, this trench could have easily accommodated another line or more. Risers themselves will be cut to size and position the sprinkler head flush with the lawn that will go in later.

When it comes time to position the first sprinkler on the first station, simply cut the PVC pipe at the appropriate point, clear out the loose dirt from around it so that it does not get inside the pipe. Keep a level within easy reach. You may want to have a few sections of precut PVC pipe sitting nearby so that you can prop up the end of the pipe that sits in the trench, so that it does not get dirt inside.

In almost all cases where you'll need to attach a sprinkler, the process is the same. Install a 'cut off' riser into the fitting, then the actual sprinkler body (containing the sprinkler nozzle) onto that. Cut off risers are generally black in color and get their name because they can be cut at nearly any location on them where there is a gap in the threads in order to achieve the correct sprinkler height.

And, in order to make sure that the sprinkler riser ends up level (perpendicular to the ground), insert a section of sprinkler riser into the fitting you are using (either the threaded T or threaded elbow) before attaching the fitting to the pipe. After you have prepared both the pipe and the fitting with primer and glue (same exact process as what was used to create the manifold a little while back), attach the fitting, and placing the level against the side of the riser (as shown in the photo below), rotate the riser until the level indicates it is perpendicular to the ground. Taking extra precautions in this process will result in properly positioned sprinklers. Sprinklers that are not positioned properly will end up tilted to one side. It looks goofy and results in a diminished reach for that sprinkler.

Though this is actually a retrofitted (repaired) sprinkler riser that had been damaged by a lawn mower, the photo below shows the method of determining if your PVC fittings (elbows, T's etc.) are level, which will also result in level sprinkler risers and of course, level sprinklers themselves.

While the above 2 photos are actually a repair and are not starting from scratch, they nevertheless show the use of a level pressed against the sprinkler riser to ensure a more level/upright installation. In the first photo, you can see that the bubble inside the level is just a little off. In the second, the fitting has been adjusted and the riser is level. This will result in more efficient coverage once the entire system is complete.

IMPORTANT – After you have finished assembling each of the sprinklers on their risers, and are satisfied with their height and alignment, leave the flags or other markers you are using in place. This will come in handy down the line, as you go to backfill your ditches. You don't want to lose sight of where your sprinklers ended up, and have to fish around for them.

MAKING TURNS

Eventually you will come to a point in the yard where a turn (even if it is less than 90 degrees) has to be made. It is likely that the ditch that will house the PVC is quite a bit wider than the PVC pipe itself, so there's room to decide just where to place that turn. How you do so depends on how many pipes are to sit side by side. If there is just the one, then it really doesn't matter, as you just need to make sure your PVC run makes the turn within the confines of the ditch.

But if there are several pipes to be positioned side by side, it becomes more important to take the time to make sure the pipes sit properly next to each other, without crossing over so that one PVC pipe ends up on top of another. A car driving over the top of the area, an inordinate amount of foot traffic, etc. and it is possible for the two pipes positioned in this manner to exert enough pressure on each other for one to crack. So, as you position the pipes for the turn, make sure that the pipe furthest from the turn itself is the longest, so that the bend is on the 'outside'. Then, each subsequent pipe can be cut to be just a bit shorter.

GETTING THE HEIGHT OF YOUR SPRINKLER HEADS RIGHT

Not only is it important to get the sprinkler risers installed nice and perpendicular to the ground so that the sprinkler ends up pointing straight, but you'll also want to make sure that when it comes time to place a sprinkler, whether it be in the middle of a PVC pipe, or at the very end of it, you get the elevation (just how far it sticks out of the ground) right. Too low and the sprinkler, even when active, will not fully REACH over a grown out lawn, resulting in inadequate coverage. Too high and you will repeatedly find it gets cut or broken by every passing lawn mower. (This, of course, will periodically happen, even when the elevation of the head is just right – just less often).

The idea is to end up with the end of the sprinkler, out of which the nozzle pops up, sitting more or less at ground level, so that when the sod or seed (whichever you decide on) is set upon it, the level of the grass is actually a little higher than the top of the sprinkler before it is engaged. This should provide enough clearance without having to worry about replacing too many sprinkler parts.

This sprinkler head is nice and flush to the ground and about 1.5-2" from the adjacent sidewalk.

PROPER PLACEMENT OF THE SPRINKLERS AT THE EDGES OF THE YARD

Just as with sprinkler height, this too is a balance of sorts. Place the sprinkler head too close to the edge of the yard, and it is likely to be in contact with a concrete driveway or sidewalk that may eventually crack it. On the other hand, position the head too far inward, and you will end up with patches of dry lawn, as the area behind the sprinkler head is not getting covered.

Try to position the edge of the sprinkler head closes to the driveway or sidewalk about 2" from it. If the head to head coverage has been computed properly based on your water pressure, this should keep everything covered and yet leave a little clearance to keep parts from breaking as often from being repeatedly walked over.

Working your way, station by station, from manifold out to the most distant sprinkler, you will eventually complete the installation of your sprinklers. Again, the process of installing 'non-lawn' sprinklers (shrub sprinklers, drip irrigation, etc.) is really the same. The only variation lies in what is actually being attached to the PVC fittings.

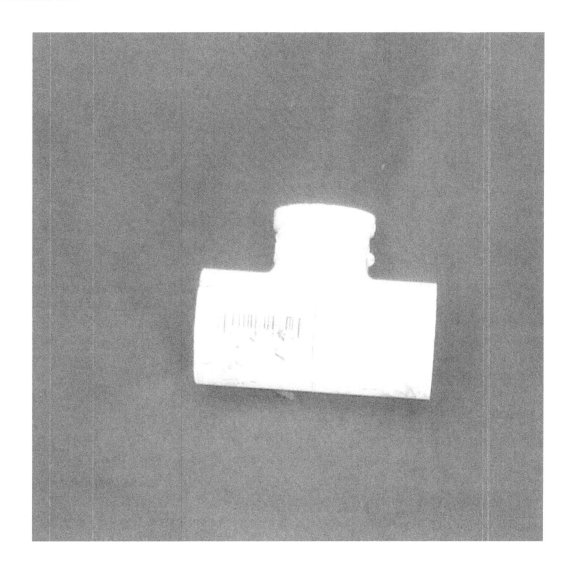

A drip system installed and in action. In this case, a flexible riser was attached to fixed riser, a four station, drip system adapter was then screwed onto the riser. You could use a longer flexible or fixed riser to do the same thing. Underneath the surface, because this is the only irrigation done by this station, a fairly short section of PVC pipe runs from the manifold to the riser via a threaded elbow, to which the riser is attached. If you were to run any additional risers, you would use a threaded "T'" on the closest riser(s) instead, followed by a threaded elbow at the most distant riser. A threaded 'T' is shown in the photo above this one.

BACKFILLING YOUR TRENCHES

Before backfilling your trenches (shoveling dirt back into the trench to get it leveled off for the lawn to follow) ALWAYS check every fitting on the PVC lines that sit inside that ditch. *Are the fittings water tight?* There's only one way to know – manually activate the sprinkler valve that controls the station you are working on to make sure. It is only after making sure that everything is operable, and that there are no leaks should you begin backfilling the ditch. It's no fun encountering a puddle on the top of your new lawn and finding it was caused by improperly glued PVC parts.

Always better to check your work and redo it where needed. You don't really want to have to go back, dig up dirt and start all over if you were to encounter leaks down the line.

Once you are sure that everything is working, then you can begin backfilling. The objective here is to try to get everything as level as possible not only on top of the ditch itself, but on either side of it. In addition, you will also want to go back over the area a few times to get the dirt compacted down into the ditch, and then water at low pressure along that area thoroughly to get it to settle even further. Otherwise, you will end up with low spots where the dirt tends to settle with time. Once the area dries, you will be able to see where you stand, and just how much additional dirt you need to get everything nice and level.

You may need to go get some top soil to add to the area to make everything is leveled out.

Just a reminder. . . make sure the locations of your sprinkler heads remain marked so that you can find them if this process causes the heads to be covered.

INSTALLING AND WIRING YOUR TIMER

This may be another area where you'll want to enlist the services of a professional. As you go to install the timer itself, there are choices you will want to make that may well determine how difficult this portion of the process is. And, because both indoor and outdoor installations will likely require drilling through a house wall, it is ***ESSENTIAL*** that you know exactly where the existing wiring in your house is routed, as you definitely do NOT want to accidentally drill into a live wire.

Having an electrician come in and outline where it is safe to drill for the routing of your sprinkler cable (from timer out to the manifold outside) will make this a LOT safer for you. If you want to go one step further and create a dedicated connection for your timer and bypass the AC adapter that comes with it to connect it to a wall socket, so much the better.

Your choices as far as timers are concerned will be determined to an extent by just how many stations you'll need. Most residential timers can accommodate are geared toward up to either a four- or a six-station configuration (no harm comes if you leave one station empty). If for some reason you find you will need more stations than that (fairly uncommon, unless we are talking about a BIG property, you would probably have to opt for what is considered a more INDUSTRIAL application.

I've always used Rain Bird timers, for the most part, and they've served me well.

Again, I have no affiliation with them. Choose your brand as you see fit. Orbit also makes residential timers that are similarly designed.

As far as find a location for the timer, as out of the way as possible, but still INSIDE the house is best.

On the other hand, it is not all that hard to position a timer outside the house – especially if you have already enlisted the services of an electrician. You will also need to choose your timer accordingly, as those intended for outside use come with their own secure enclosure to protect them from the elements, while those for inside use do not.

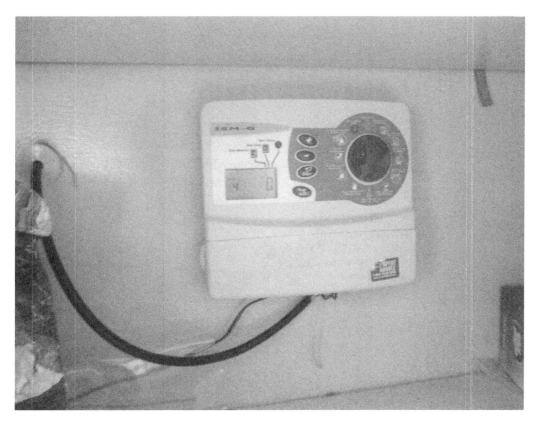

There really isn't a good way to make a sprinkler timer look aesthetically pleasing, so generally the idea is to position them as far out of view as possible. Here we see a couple of possibilities - behind bedroom furniture and right inside a kitchen cabinet. In the case of the latter, the grommet seen at the left of the timer will be affixed to the wall, creating a more airtight seal.

While in the case of the first position, an AC outlet happened to be very close by and also out of sight, such adapters are, of course, not generally found inside kitchen cabinets. Because of this, it was necessary to drill a small hole through the cabinet so that the AC adapter could be plugged in underneath and then connected.

Once you have decided where you want your timer to be located, you will want to secure it in place and then run your wiring from the timer to the manifold, allowing electrical current can reach your automatic valves.

Nearly any residential timer will generally come with its own mounting hardware. For our purposes, we'll assume you went with an inside installation. So, the timer would generally come with two or more mounting screws to secure it in place. When installing these screws, be sure to double check your work, so that the locations of the screws are nice and level – which will in turn result in your timer being level when you are done.

With an interior installation, you will also want to make sure the location you have decided on is close enough to an A/C outlet so that the A/C adapter provided with the timer can reach from a wall socket to the timer itself. That is, unless you decide to enlist the services of an electrician to hardwire your timer. The latter makes for a nicer looking finish, but is not essential to the proper running of the timer or your system. The A/C adapter that comes with the timer will generally last a LONG time and is pretty fail safe.

CAUTION: Drilling a hole into the exterior wall in order to route your wiring from the timer to the manifold can be potentially dangerous, as you could conceivably come in contact with a LIVE electrical wire. At best, this could damage your house's electrical system. At worst, potentially lethal injuries could occur. ***DIYSprinklerbook assumes no responsibility for injuries or other consequences that may result from drilling in this manner. I strongly recommend that you enlist the services of a professional to determine where it is safe to drill, or have them complete this step.***

Whether you do this yourself, or enlist the services of a professional, the required hole to route the sprinkler cable from inside to outside should be located as close by as possible, so that you don't have unnecessary lengths running through your cabinet, across a wall, or wherever you decided to mount the timer. In order to minimize the amount of air that may seep in around the hole, you'll want to get 2 rubber grommets (one for the inside wall, one for the outside wall) that will affix to the cable itself and can then be bonded to the respective walls. When you are ready to wire the timer, you will just slide the cable through this grommet, with the flat portion of the grommet then affixed to the wall surrounding the hole that has been drilled for the cable. This will make for a more attractive and insulated installation.

With the timer securely mounted in place using the provided screws affixed to the interior wall, it is time to wire your system.

Sprinkler cable, like timers, come in several denominations, based on the number of valves you are going to need to connect. The cable itself consists of a thick, usually black, insulated housing that contains smaller colored wire inside. Each of these colored wires contained inside will connect first to your timer (where a tension screw is generally clearly marked from 1 – 6, assuming a six station timer) to a corresponding sprinkler valve. In addition, you will also see a white wire that will act as a ground – again, both inside at the timer and outside at the manifold.

In order for the timer to function properly, each end must correspond the same numbered station, so that electricity is routed to the solenoid – giving the command for the valve to open and let water through. In order to minimize trips back and forth, from inside to outside the house, bring a pad with you once the timer in installed, marking down what color you are mounting to each station. For example: #1 blue, #2 red, #3 black, #4 green, #5 yellow and #6 orange (again, assuming a six station timer) before you go outside to do the same.

To get this process started, you will want to make sure that the sprinkler cable has been passed through the hole that has been drilled through the wall, and can reach the timer without too many twists and turns. Once it is in place, you will want to first take a set of wire strippers (PICTURED) and strip off a length of the black insulation that covers the outside of the wire – maybe 2-3" worth, so that the colored wires contained inside can be separated and make their way to each of the tension screws that correspond to the timer stations they will run.

Next, you will also want to strip each of the colored wires, leaving about 1.5" of exposed metal. *Again – as you begin, working from tension screw #1 onward, be sure and write down the color used for each station, so that as you go back outside, you will know what color will attach to which solenoid head to complete the connection.*

Loosen each of the tension screws slowly, as they are not generally set inside the timer all that far, and you don't want one to go flying out of reach. (*They are not as easy of a replacement as you might think*). You will want to take the exposed metal portion of each of the colored wires, and bend it carefully around the tension screw to form a secure connection, before again tightening the tension screw down onto the wire. For safety sake, use gloves as you do this and make sure you have not yet plugged in the AC adapter that comes with the timer.

Once each of the colored wires has been tensioned into place, you will then want to do the same with the white ground cable, fastening it down in the position indicated. This wire will connect in the same fashion, but to the tension screw clearly marked "ground".

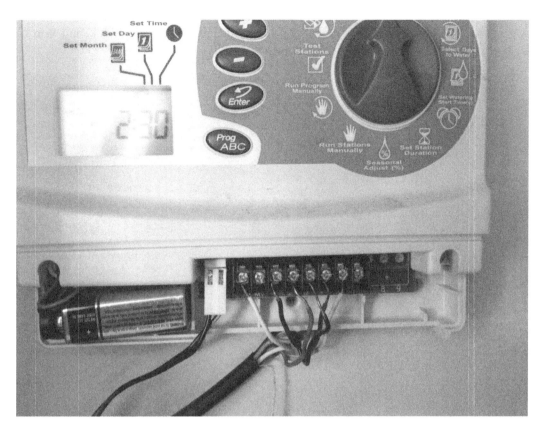

As you can see here, the individual wires contained in a spool of sprinkler wire are color coded. Unlike most such wires, they do not consist of a multitude of thin, wispy strands, but are one solid and somewhat thicker strand each. On this end, each of them is connected to the timer via individual set screws. The white cable on the leftmost set screw is the ground wire.

Once this end is finished, and you are satisfied with the positioning of the cable as it runs from the timer, out the hole in the wall to the outdoors where it will meet up with the manifold, you can then slide the grommet into place against the wall, and fasten it with either glue or contact cement (very carefully placed, of course, so as not to stain the exterior of your house).

With the inside portion of the wiring now finished, it is time to move outside to where the sprinkler cable exists the house and extends downward to the manifold. You may find that the contrast of a black sprinkler cable against a lighter colored house isn't a great visual, so you can either paint the cable itself the same color your house, or you can purchase a plastic channel that can affix to the side of the house (ideally painted to match the side of the house) and place the cable inside as it runs to the manifold). If you opt for the latter, make sure you use a level to get the channel to run straight down vertically.

Make sure you have adjusted the cable so that there is very little slack and yet no tension as it runs down to the manifold. As you bring the cable to the manifold, be careful not to cut off the excess cabling so that it doesn't reach the individual solenoid heads. You can always go back and cut more cable off if you find you have too much slack, but you can't go back and add cable if your connection runs short.

Here we can see the cable running out to the manifold. In this case, the cable itself has been texture coated and matches the exterior finish of the house. It can be affixed to the exterior wall by using an appropriate adhesive. As an alternative, you can also go to the lighting department of your home improvement store and buy some 'raceway', plastic chutes that are shaped to hold and conceal wiring. The raceway can be attached to the wall, and then painted to match.

Once you are satisfied with the positioning of the cable, and are confident that you have left enough of it to reach where it needs to (being sure that you have left some slack so that there is no tension on the wires themselves as they connect to the solenoid heads), you can then cut off the excess cable as you see fit.

It's worth repeating . . . Leave enough slack so that each of the wires inside can easily reach their destination on the tops of the solenoids. After having done so, you will want to strip off a more substantial length of the black cable insulation (maybe 8" or so), so that the colored wires contained inside can be spread out to reach each of the solenoid heads that sit atop the manifold.

Keeping your list that gives the corresponding color for each station within easy reach, you will now strip each of the colored cables so that they can be attached.

As you do so, you will notice that each of the solenoids that sits atop each valve has TWO wires running out of the top. One of these is to accommodate the colored wire that connects it to its corresponding numbered position on the timer, and the other is to accommodate a common ground wire that will also connect one wire each from the remaining solenoids to a common connection.

As these wires are not purpose-specific (nor positive/negative), it does not matter which wire you select off each of the solenoids to be a ground or to affix the colored wire, just so long as the connections are secure.

To complete these connections, you can either use plastic threaded cap connections (readily available in the electrical section of your home improvement store), black electrical tape or gel caps. The latter will provide a water proof seal and is less prone to falling off the wire connection than are caps.

Here is the other end of the sprinkler wiring - the end that will connect to each of the solenoid tops on the valves. From here, it's just a matter of making sure you keep track of the color wire you are using for each station, beginning with the attachments at the set screws.

Keep moving forward by completing each connection based on its corresponding color (again #1 may be blue, #2 red, etc.). Once you are finished with this, you can then strip the white wire, and connect it to the ground wires you have selected from each of the solenoid caps.

As you can see, each of our anti-siphon valves has two wires coming out of the solenoid cap. One is used for a ground, the other to be connected to the live wire, the color of which should correspond to the other end that is attached to the timer. These 2 wires are NON-SPECIFIC, meaning that it does not matter which you choose for ground or live, provided that both connections are made.

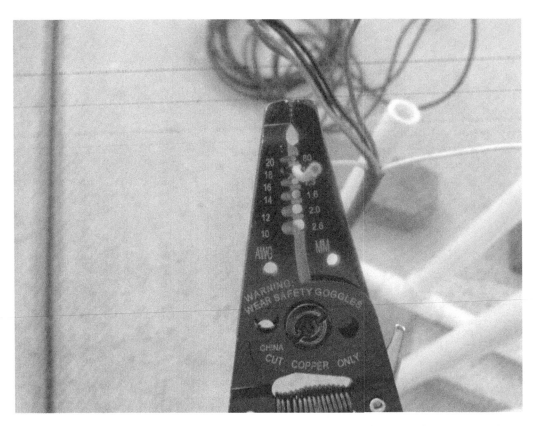

This 2 in one wire stripper/cutter allows us to both cut wires to size, and then strip their outer insulation to make connections with the caps shown in the next photo. In the case of the wires coming out of the solenoid heads, you may want to cut just a little more off than what they come with, in order to make connections a little more solid.

Here we see the live wires from our three anti-siphon valves wired up to the sprinkler wire. It's a good idea to double check that the connections have been made to the correct valves, with colors matching at both ends (timer and solenoid). The exposed wire will be covered with electrical tape for added protection from the elements.

The ground wire is now attached to the other three remaining solenoid wires. In most cases, even with a six station manifold there is enough ground wire to get all the wires gathered in one place. However, if you find differently, you can always create a 'bridge' wire. Just cut off a length of white (ground) wire from the remainder of the sprinkler wire (and there is almost always extra) strip it as needed, and create a ground 'bridge' by connecting three solenoid ground wires to each end with caps. One end must then also be connected to the ground wire coming out of the house.

While there is usually enough wire length provided on each of the solenoid caps, occasionally, as with a six station manifold, or a manifold whose valves are situated fairly far apart, you may not be able to get all of the ground wires to meet at one location to be connected to the corresponding white ground wire coming out of the sprinkler cable.

If this is the case, you can instead cut out a section of the discarded, excess sprinkler cable, take out the white wire inside, strip both ends, and connect one end to a set of three or so ground wires from one end of the manifold, and then connect the other end to the remaining valves. The connection closest to the cable coming out of the house can then be connected to the white ground wire inside the sprinkler cable.

With everything now connected, you will want to test your system, using your timer's 'manual mode' to make sure all the connections are solid, no connections have been crossed from inside to outside the house to the wrong station, etc. To do this properly, you'll want to VISUALLY check and see that the correct station has been activated. Don't merely take the sound of your sprinkler stations activating as a sign everything is okay. An improperly connected valve – for example if you were to connect station #2 to the #3 on the manifold- will still activate a valve, just not the one you are planning on.

In other words, even if you were to accidentally cross wires – connecting say, the blue wire to the Station #1 tension screw inside and then to Station #3 outside, you would HEAR a station being activated, but it would be the wrong station. So, make sure you having another look to make sure that everything is being activated as you planned.

For most timers, the method of manual testing is pretty self-explanatory – for the Rain Bird timers for example, you will usually see a setting clearly marked "operate valves manually". You can just move the control knob to this setting, then follow the prompts on the screen to input 1-2 minutes of time for each station to activate. This should provide enough time for you to have a look outside and make sure everything is running properly.

This will also be a good time to re-check the coverage of each of your sprinkler heads.

As the contrast of wet and dry dirt on a lawn yet to be planted is pretty easy to see. Once each station has been allowed to run for a couple of minutes, it should be fairly evident (from the saturated ground), where the spray radius of each sprinkler head is reaching. This coverage should be about the same (varying only because of wind conditions) as it was when you checked your work before digging your trenches for your PVC pipe.

In the event you do find that your coverage has changed since before you installed the timer and checked it manually, often the culprit is the timer setting, as many timers have an additional setting allowing you to restrict the water flow to the sprinklers if you desire.

Another place to look would be at the main bypass valve (the T-fitting you had installed at the beginning of the process to allow the water flow to your system to be turned on and off without affecting the flow inside your house). Make sure this valve is all the way open, or at the very least as close to it as you need to get the sprinkler head coverage you planned on.

Once you have run each station in your timer's manual mode to check ground coverage, while allowing each valve to activate properly on its own a couple of times. It's time to move on to the next step.

ADDING YOUR LAWN, PLANTS, VEGETABLES/FRUIT, ETC.

So, what did you decide on – sod or seed?

Both have their advantages and disadvantages.

In either case, no matter which you choose, weather may be a consideration.

Freezing conditions will kill grass seed before it has a chance to germinate, so if you are in a part of the country that sustains such weather, you will not want to plant during the dead of winter. Certain varieties of seed are more acclimated to cold weather than others, but none of them can be planted in freezing conditions.

On the other hand, smoldering hot weather can also stop the growing process in its tracks, but in most cases, the weather would have to be fairly extremely (as in continuous temperatures in the 90's or above) to have this effect.

SOD VS. SEED: PROS AND CONS
SOD
Pros to Using Sod
With all the work you will have put in up to this point, there's certainly nothing wrong with a little instant gratification – the ability to **INSTANTLY** see the results of your labor. This is what sod provides. When the area is properly prepped and the sod is properly installed, sod grows almost immediately. And when you finish laying down that last piece of sod, you have that definitive proof that the installation phase of this project is, for the most part, finished.

Once the sod has grown some – which happens pretty quickly if climate matches the variety you have chosen– in about 7-10 days your lawn will be ready to be mowed. The seams that may look obvious as you are laying down the sod actually fill up and you are left with a nice, green carpet of lawn. No waiting for the grass seed to germinate. No waiting for the initially stringy sprigs of grass to grow to their mature state. Not much worrying about weeds growing out of the ground faster than the grass seeds do. (This may still happen, just not nearly to the extent that it does when using seed.)

Yep. Nice solid lawn.

Laying down sod is certainly more work than merely broadcasting (spreading) seed. You'll want to get some Amend, or another form sod starter, to spread and work into the top of the ground to speed the growth of the sod and to help it take root (knit) faster. (Another reason to consider purchasing a rototiller, as opposed to renting one). And of course, as you place each strip of sod, you will want to make sure that each piece is right up against the other (but not so tight that the edges are buckling, which will guarantee at least some of the sod quickly browns and dies).

In order to make sure each piece of sod is set firmly against the ground beneath it, and to avoid the aforementioned air pockets that will cause brown, dead spots above wherever they occur, you'll need to go out and rent a sod roller (basically a large, rolling cylinder that you will fill with water to add weight to) to further compact the bottom of each sod piece into the soil below, so that you can eliminate these air pockets and get the growing started.

While more difficult than merely spreading seed, in all, laying down sod is not that difficult a task- if you pace yourself correctly. Working alone, and not at a breakneck piece, I can get 100 – 120 pieces properly prepped and situated, taking most of one day, and without getting too exhausted. You may be able to do better, and if you can enlist the help of others, the area you are able to cover will multiply. Just to give you an idea of how much progress this equates to, each piece of sod is generally 15" wide by 4' long. So, if you were to put down 100 pieces in a yard say, 40' wide, you would end up with 40' by about 12 ½' covered.

The upside is undeniable. Just install the sod properly, and get started right away with a proper watering schedule – which generally means thoroughly soaking, though not drowning, the lawn upon planting it, watering three times a day (all before 4pm, where city regulations allow) for the first week, tailing that down to two times a day for the next week, and then daily (preferably in the morning) for the third and fourth week, before ultimately going to a schedule of once every 2-3 days after that.

Pretty easy stuff, really.

Somewhere between Pro and Con - Price

To give you an idea of price, you will generally find that home improvement stores offer sod strips for around 2.00 – 2.20 – with each piece being 15" x 4'. So, that 40'x 12.5' plot we referred to would end up costing you around $200-220. Not a King's ransom, but a not inconsequential amount, either – especially if you have a fairly large yard to cover.

Cons to Using Sod
Lack of sod variety.

One of the other drawbacks with sod is there just are not all that many varieties offered. Go to any home improvement store, and you are likely to find fescue . . . . and not much else. Fescue is certainly a good looking lawn, probably my favorite, but it does have its drawbacks – it doesn't do its best during extended periods of warm weather and will tend to turn brown . . . or worse.

Versatility (As the result of that lack of variety)

Not all fescue is treated equal. Highly controlled growing conditions and experimentation have resulted in fescue that can be more drought resistant, more heat resistant, more durable in high traffic areas, and perhaps most relevant, can tolerate shade.

The amount of shade your yard gets is certainly going to be a consideration anyway. For the most part, any portion of your yard that does not get at least 3-4 hours of direct sunlight each day will probably not support a lawn.

The reason is simple – no sunlight, no photosynthesis.

Next time you head down to your home improvement store, have a look at the seed variations that are offered. You will see some that say specifically 'shade tolerant', or something similar. While this variety will not tolerate exposure to ***nothing*** but shade, it will generally do a little better than that 3-4-hour range mentioned earlier. So, even if you have a patch of lawn that sees little sun, or is perhaps dominated by a tree that, while looking nice, overshadows (literally) the lawn, this shade tolerant seed may just make a lawn viable in such conditions.

By contrast, nearly all sod is grown in direct sunlight, and is, as a result, not all that shade tolerant. So, if your property doesn't see a lot of sunlight, sod may not be a viable choice.

LET'S ASSUME YOU CHOOSE SOD. HERE'S HOW TO INSTALL IT.

If your yard is fairly appreciable in size, you are probably going to be best off getting your sod delivered, as opposed to borrowing or renting a pickup truck (assuming you don't have one of your own, of course) and venturing on down to the home improvement store. This is for two reasons:

The store may not have sufficient quantity – Home improvement stores generally order a predetermined amount of sod from a variety of their providers. And once that sod is delivered, it's up for grabs for all of their shoppers. On some days that pile of sod may appear to be nearly untouched, while on other days it's long gone by 12noon. No point in planning your day around this project, only to find that you are only able to come back home with a few pieces of sod to install.

Sod degrades fairly quickly. You are generally advised to put down your sod as soon as possible after you either purchase / take possession of it. A few minutes or even an hour won't make much of a difference, but over the course of a day, especially in hot weather, sod wilts and degrades pretty fast. As many home improvement stores display their sod facing directly into the sun, without keeping it watered, before you make your purchase, this is something to watch out for.

Have another look. This is why you may not want to merely venture down to your home improvement store and take your chances with what they have in stock. When the dirt bed that nourishes the sod dries out, the same may well be for the sod itself. For more limited quantities, as would be the case in fixing a dead patch, etc., you are probably fine going this route, as you can cherry pick through the inventory.

A better way? Pre-order what you need (or more specifically, what you are capable of installing in one day) and have it delivered. Especially if that order is going to be 100 pieces (each piece/strip is 4ft x 15"). This is usually the minimum order for free delivery. So, if your yard is something on the order of 36' wide x 15' deep, for example, that is going to require 108 pieces of sod, just a little over that minimum *(9 pieces across by 12 pieces deep)*.

Even if you are not able to make that minimum, it may still be worth it to have your sod delivered. You are going to be making enough trips back and forth from the sod pile to your yard and a good delivery service will offload your order, generally with a small forklift, and put it pretty much wherever you want it. Saves a lot of time, and the fee, assuming a smaller order, is generally not that bad.

There are usually two ways to order – one from your home improvement store and the other from an actual sod provider. In the case of the latter, you may again come up against order minimums, but if that is not the issue, it may be better to go ahead and order from the provider. For example, here in Southern California, Southland Sod is a reputable company to work with. And they often are the ones that supply sod to the home improvement stores anyway.

WORDS OF CAUTION!! – If you do order from a sod supplier and you don't buy an order sufficient to cover your lawn in one delivery, ALWAYS make sure the second order you make is coming from the same sod farm as the first. The reason? Uniformity. Variations in climate and soil conditions, even slight ones, will result in grass that has a subtle difference in appearance. And you do not want that. I am speaking from personal experience on this one.

When ordering from a sod grower/provider, you will generally receive your deliver on pallets, as the delivery usually includes offload via forklift from a semi-truck.

PREPPING FOR SOD

Before the sod arrives, you should have your plot of land all ready for it. That means going through one last time to make sure you are rid of weeds, that the land is level, thoroughly settled but not compacted and shaped as you want it.

Once you are there, you will want to work some sod prep/starter fertilizer (also used for seed cover, if you go that route) into the soil at a depth of about 1" or so. Unlike regular fertilizers, starter fertilizer is generally high in phosphorus, but lower in nitrogen, so it won't burn the roots of that newly planted sod.

Make sure whatever you are using does not contain herbicide. Just as herbicide prevents weeds from taking hold and growing, it will also prevent grass from growing, so that your sod may not take root, and eventually dry up and die out. It'll be quite a while before you can apply any weed-killing products (somewhere after the third or fourth mowing of the lawn, in most cases).

INSTALLATION

With the starter fertilizer worked into the soil, and the soil settled enough and graded how you want it, I find it useful to get the ground just a little bit wet – not enough so that the soil gets swampy, as that will result in an uneven lawn, but enough so that, for example, dust does not kick up when you lay down each piece of sod.

Starting from the most distant corner of the lawn and work in whatever direction is LONGEST. When I get to the end of that line of sod pieces – probably arriving at a sidewalk or driveway, I then use a carpenter's square (an L-shaped metallic or wooden straight edge), lay it down where that ending is, and cut across it with a sharp knife. In doing this, try not to leave a gap between the edge of the sod and the sidewalk or driveway (doesn't look good) or the opposite – avoid trying to stuff too much sod into a space not big enough to accommodate it. If you do the latter, it will almost certainly cause the piece of sod to buckle, and allow air to get between the sod and the ground underneath. This will also cause the sod to die out.

Just as when building a brick wall, you don't want each of your rows to have parallel seams. Too much potential for air to get underneath and kill the sod. So, stagger your rows. Once the first row is finished, start the next row with a half piece (again, using the square to cut a strip of sod into even halves) so that the first seam lands somewhere in the middle of the corresponding piece 'above' it. Just like a brick wall. Obviously, in order to stagger the seams between the rows like this, you will have to cut some of the sod strips in half – again, same principle as with a brick wall. It's fairly important that the cut pieces have edges that will fit closely to the strip nearest, so you will want to make sure these cuts are done as close to 90 degrees as possible. To do this, use a square (a metallic or plastic "L" shaped instrument that allows you to cut in a perpendicular fashion, as opposed to just free-handing it. This way, you won't end up with gaps between the seams. Just take a strip of sod, make sure one edge of the square is even with a long side of the strip (which should create a perpendicular edge across the strip) and cut across with a utility knife.

Once a few rows are complete, you'll to take the sod roller out and go over the area already completed to compress the newly-placed sod into the ground, eliminate air pockets and provide a nice solid surface for the roots of the sod to attach themselves to the ground underneath. Make sure that sod roller is FILLED with water to make it its absolute heaviest. It won't kill the grass, but it will give you a better result - less of a chance of die off from air pockets forming underneath the sod than if you just lightly go over the sod with a lighter roller.

I generally prefer to start placing that very first piece of sod at the most distant point of the yard from where the sod pile is situated, only because I figure on being more fatigued as the day rolls on, and it just seems more practical to save the shorter trips back and forth from sod pile to installation location for later.

FINISHING OFF YOUR WORK

After you have placed all the strips of sod possible on the more or less rectangular area of the yard, you can get to work on the areas that have curves, or other irregular shapes. When working with more or less perpendicular surfaces, it makes sense to use a straight edge – preferably a metallic ruler or something similar – to act as a guide for your cutting. When you are working on a curved area, you don't have this luxury. Instead, I prefer to place the piece of sod with as many adjoining sides as possible positioned where you want them to be – neither leaving a gap nor stacking against the nearest piece so tightly it causes buckling or gapping, and then placing a knee on top of the strip as close to the irregular edge as possible, CAREFULLY sinking the knife or cutting instrument you are using into the sod piece as near to the border that gives the edge its curve, and slowly (and again CAREFULLY) trace the edge with the knife to correspond to the edge you are working with.

Once you have everything covered with sod as you like, I'd recommend going back over the entire yard with the sod roller. Everyone once in a while, as you try to position piece after piece as snugly as possible to the piece next to it, some shifting can occur, and this can throw larger areas out of alignment.

WATERING – Time is of the essence
It may seem that sod that is pretty sturdy stuff. To an extent, it is. But leave it exposed to a lot of heat and direct sunlight and it can start to degrade pretty easily. ***Especially if it is not kept wet.*** So, if you are working on an especially hot day, or if you find yourself taking longer than you had anticipated, or if you SEE the sod pile starting to dry out, get some water on it as soon as possible. In extreme cases, it may even be a good idea to cover the pile with wet towels to keep the moisture in (but only if you anticipate finishing everything up relatively quickly, not leaving the pile covered as is for a long period of time, which can also cause some damage from lack of exposure to sunlight.

You'll want to stop periodically to lightly water the sod pieces already in position, as drying can also occur in that position as well. And when that happens, the corners of the sod tend to curl upwards, letting air in, and causing damage.

Once you are finished positioning the sod as you want it, you are now ready to get the watering schedule going for your new lawn. As you should have already finished positioning, wiring and programming your timer, this can now be done automatically. Even before you get to this point, however, it is generally a good idea to make sure the entire lawn is pretty thoroughly soaked (not marshy), as this helps accelerate the start of the growth process, getting the roots of the sod to grow downward toward the moisture to attach to the soil underneath.

Just a recap of the recommended watering schedule for newly placed sod. This is assuming fescue is used, but is also applicable for many other major sod types. Also, outside temperature plays a big part in terms of how much water is needed and how fast it will evaporate, so use this only as a guideline:

- 2-3 times per day for the first week or so, (stretched out from early morning to mid-day). Depending on the weather and wind conditions, maybe for 6-8 minutes per area/station, maybe a little longer if you are experiencing extreme heat or a lot of wind.

- 1 time per day after maybe the first 10 days, with the same duration

- Every other day, same general duration, by the third week.

- After around the third to fourth week, water as needed.

Again, this information is a GENERAL overview. Your watering requirements will no doubt vary depending on your weather, soil conditions, etc.

Unless you are in an area where nights are relatively warm, watering should generally be done during the day . . . not at night. When watering at night, except in warmer weather, moisture may sit on top of the leaves for a long time, maybe even hours. In cooler climates, this can lead to a fungus-infested lawn. It's usually better if the grass blades themselves are dry when nighttime comes.

In some areas of the country, such as Los Angeles, certain restricts have been put on watering due to drought conditions. In these cases, watering may not be allowed after 9a or before 4p, so you will want to plan accordingly.

SIGNS THAT YOU ARE OVERWATERING (OR UNDERWATERING))
If water collects at the surface level of your sod and doesn't readily drain, you should definitely plan on watering for a little less time the next time around.

The best way to assess things is by checking the soil just below the surface of the sod – maybe for the first 1" down or so. It should be moist, but not completely wet underneath.

By contrast, if you run the same test, but you don't find that a depth of approximately 1" remains moist (not wet), then you should increase the watering duration by just a little bit.

So, in summary, sod does offer several great benefits you just can't get with seed – quicker, more obvious results being the most obvious. But supposing you decide not to go this way . . .

SEED
Pros to Using Seed
Cost
If cost is a primary consideration, seed wins out over sod pretty handily. For under $40, you can buy a 20lb bag of fescue seed at most home improvement stores that will cover nearly 1000 square feet. Not bad at all. And certainly, because of the low cost, there is no issue in having to periodically re-seed, which is going to be pretty much inevitable anyway.

Add in the cost of seed cover (maybe $4 a bag – with 7-8 bags covering that 1000 square feet pretty handily) and the cost of renting a manure spreader (a mesh cylinder perforated to release a controlled amount of seed cover as you roll it across your lawn) and you have pretty much everything you need at a pretty decent price.

Variety
If you are looking for something other than fescue, seed is going to be a hands-down winner over sod. A number of grass varieties are available in this forum – rye, bluegrass, Bermuda, mixtures, etc. And if you are looking for fescue, there are several varieties readily

available nearly everywhere that will allow you to do a better job of matching your lawn to the conditions it will grow in.

Cons to Using Seed
Time

Certainly, it takes an appreciable amount of time for seed to germinate, grow strong and attain the appearance of an attractive lawn. Depending on conditions, this time may range from weeks to several months. To some, this is not an extraordinary amount of time to wait, but choosing seed just doesn't give you the nearly instant gratification that sod provides.

The Need for 'Do-Overs'

Even under the best of circumstances, and no matter how careful you are, you will have some patches on your lawn where seed simply doesn't grow (germinate) on the first try. Could have been that the seed in that area had been exposed to some moisture, but not enough to allow it to germinate. Perhaps the seed was not distributed as generously in that area. Maybe the soil was not quite as well prepared. I have also seen many instances where, the seed has simply been buried too far below the surface, because the seed cover was applied too thick and remains dormant.

Regardless of how carefully you plan and execute, you'll need to be prepared to go back over some of those areas 1-2 times before seeds start to sprout and your lawn is on its way.

One of the drawbacks to using seed is the inevitability that you will have a 'do-over' or two to get full coverage. Here, you can see that, despite the thickness of the surrounding areas, there are some bare spots that will require more attention.

Weeds

No matter how careful you were when applying Roundup, or whatever other product you chose to use, as grass seed is beginning to germinate and sprout from the ground, weeds will almost certainly begin to crop as well. When this happens, initially you will be able tempted to step lightly across your newly growing lawn and carefully pluck the weeds out, but eventually, you will run into a time where the lawn is not quite ready for 'weed and feed' type products and yet, you start to see weeds becoming more prevalent.

Another drawback to using seed is the tendency for weeds to crop up in substantial quantities before the germinated grass is mature enough to withstand any 'weed and feed' products. You just have to have some patience and avoid spending unnecessary time pulling weed after weed, or risking the damage such products may do when applied too soon.

Resist the temptation to spend what would eventually become a lot of time trying to pick each and every weed out individually, and instead rely on adopting a regular, sound fertilizing program using quality products, such as *Vigoro* or *Scotts*, but only ***ONCE THE LAWN IS GROWN OUT ENOUGH TO HANDLE THESE PRODUCTS***. This is very important, as applying virtually any weed-killing product (even one that states on the label that it won't harm grass) prematurely can end up killing your new lawn.

Both of these companies, as well as other brands, feature products that are geared toward application at particular times of the year – times when certain weeds are most apt to pop up, when insects are an issue, etc. When you follow the instructions not only as far as how much to apply, but WHEN to apply it, you will be able to spend more time ENJOYING the look of your lawn, and less time in a crouching position trying to keep it weed free.

APPLYING SEED PROPERLY

In order to end up with a nice, even, professional looking lawn, you will want to take extra care to broadcast (spread) seed evenly during its application. On any bag of seed you buy, fairly specific instructions as to how to apply the product are prominently featured. One thing you will want to be sure of is that the brand of seed spread you BUY (these are not generally featured for rent, so you will either need to purchase or borrow from a neighbor) is a model named in the instructions. While it may seem a little counterintuitive, most brands of spreaders, even major brands, are calibrated just a little differently from each other, and this can make a pronounced difference as to just how much seed is laid down in a given area.

Take this part of the process nice and slowly. As you walk the area behind the spreader, be sure you are working in straight (and slightly overlapping) rows. The contrast of the fairly pale grass seeds against the much darker ground below them will provide ample evidence as to how much seed is coming out of the spreader and just where it is going. When you run out of seed inside the spreader and have to 'reload' from the bag of seed, it's a good idea to leave the spreader where you last left off, and bring the bag to the spreader to refill, as opposed to wheeling the spreader across the yard (which will make it hard to remember where you left off and may displace some grass seed).

WHAT TO EXPECT FROM YOUR LAWN AT THIS POINT

So, at this point, regardless of whether you chose to go with seed or sod, you should eventually have a tangible lawn to maintain, and a functioning automatic sprinkler system to go along with it.

If you went with sod, the seams between the individual pieces will fade over time, resulting in a lawn that becomes one seamless, continuous piece of green growth, if the right conditions are maintained.

If you went with grass seed, and assuming the conditions you provided are optimal, you should see growth fairly soon after planting (7-12 days, usually), though this does depend on weather, to an extent.

PLANTS, VEGETABLES, FRUIT, ETC.

More often than not, a finished yard not only consists of a lawn, but also flowerbeds, perhaps even a vegetable garden.

As was covered previously during the 'installation' phase, each of these variations will require their own irrigation application, which should be in place well BEFORE planting. If you are planting flowers, assuming that the shrub sprinklers have been tested and cover what they are supposed to, a properly designed flower bed makes a big difference. I am certainly no florist, but some obvious tips. . .

Make sure that plants in close proximity have the same watering and shade needs. This may mean placing one variety of plant right next to another where, despite their proximity, the amount of shade reaching each is a factor.

When purchasing plants, read the instructions on the label. This will show the finished height, width, watering schedule and shade needs of that plant. It looks amateurish to place overly tall plants in front of shorter plants behind them, because it will ultimately obscure the view you have to the shorter plants. Same thing if plants are crowded too close together.

Make sure you are placing the plants with proper depth, and not outside the reach of the shrub sprinklers being used to irrigation the flower bed.

VEGETABLES, FRUITS, ETC.

As noted above, these also will require specialized irrigation, which should also already be in place before planting. Often, in a limited area, it will require only one sprinkler riser being fitted with an adapter that will allow it to service several fruit or vegetable plants via a drip system. Be sure to use Teflon tape for this purpose as well.

There are a variety of specialized 'converter' heads that will allow you to do this. They are usually available in 4, 6 or 12 location varieties, meaning that 4, 6 or 12 micro-tubes can be attached, which will then branch out so that they terminate at the base of the plant that they are irrigating.

4 micro-tube converter head attached to a flexible riser. The photo on right shows a button dripper providing irrigation to a tomato plant. This is set up to avoid wetting the leaves of the plant, which are very prone to mildew.

If you are planning on situating a lot of fruit or vegetable plants in one location, you will want to take heed to the previous instruction – make sure that they all have the same approximate watering needs. Otherwise, you may well find some of them end up with too much water, where others end up with too little.

Also, assuming (for example) that you are placing 12 fruit or vegetable plants in one area, I would recommend planning on using several micro-tube converters, each with perhaps 4 micro-tubes connected, as opposed to purchasing the available 12 micro-tube converters. The latter, in my experience, do not feature as sturdy of a connection between the cap and the micro-tube, causing the micro-tube to frequently become dislodged when the station servicing it is activated. Just my opinion.

This lawn has been allowed to completely grow out until viable for mowing. The high spots you see in the center are pretty common, as some portions of the lawn likely germinated well before others. You can see that the weeds at lower left have not become much more pronounced, and can now be treated with the appropriate product. Needless to say, make sure you don't use Roundup for this purpose, but rather a product that will kill the weed while sparing the lawn.

The same lawn has been allowed to mature a bit more, and has been mowed. Note the substantially darker color.

THE HARD PART IS DONE!!

Certainly any lawn will require maintenance. Weeds will eventually crop up. Soil may become compacted. You may experience some mildew during the times of the year where sunlight is less plentiful. All of these will require some attention so that they are controlled before becoming a bigger problem.

A couple of the more common issues you will have to deal with:

Broken Sprinkler Riser – If you see a pronounced area where the grass is marshy and does not drain between watering sessions. This is likely the culprit. Perhaps a gardener (maybe even YOU) clipped the sprinkler head just hard enough to put a small split in the riser. This is easily remedied with the kit that was described toward the opening of this E-book.

Here, we are using an extractor (T-handle is visible) to remove a broken sprinkler riser. While the photo shown is a flower bed, this is also a common cause of swampy spots on a lawn as well.

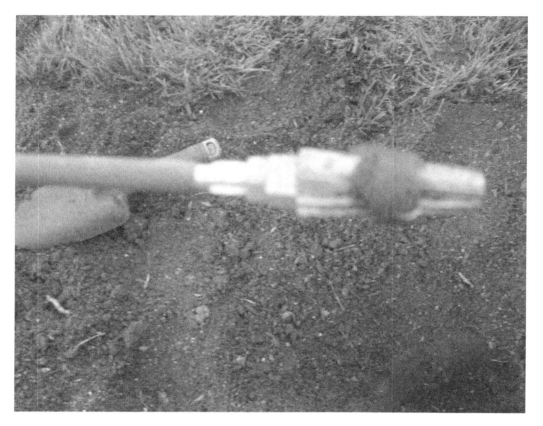

The broken portion has been extracted and sits on the extractor tool. Now, we can easily just replace the riser with another one, cut to the appropriate size.

Broken PVC Pipe- It's a lot less common. . .luckily, because it's also a lot more time and labor intensive to fix. A break or crack in PVC pipes or fittings is indicated by an even more pronounced saturated area. In extreme cases, enough water pressure can accumulate to even lift a well-established layer of sod so that it looks like a blister. If you do end up encountering this, you will want to start by isolating the area where the break is. This is done by establishing where the grass is marshiest. From there, there really is no alternative but to dig up inside a perimeter where you suspect the break or crack may be. Good thing trenches are generally only 10-12".   Once you find the break, it can be repaired as follows:

Isolate and cut out the break. In this particular case, you can see the jagged edge at the left. This will need to be cut more even with a set of PVC cutters. You will need to make sure you make the cut large enough so that the PVC repair piece (shown in the next photo) easily fits between the two pieces, where it can then be manually 'telescoped' out to fit snugly after applying PVC primer and cement – just as you would do with any other PVC connection.

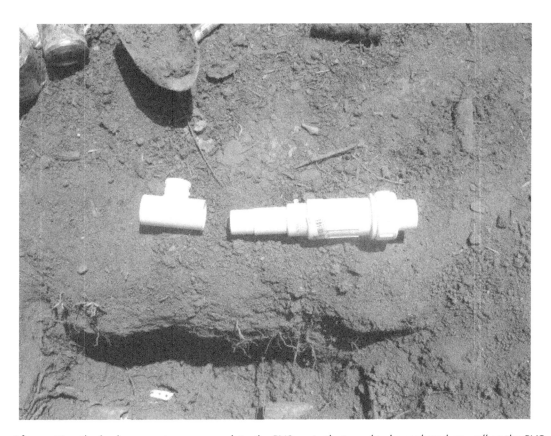

After cutting the broken area to accommodate the PVC parts that need to be replaced, as well as the PVC patch, lay out your replacement part so that you can make sure your measurements were correct. In this case, you see a threaded 'T' that held a sprinkler riser, along with a telescoping PVC patch that will allow us to fix the break without having to dig up an appreciable length of PVC pipe.

The completed repair. This was accomplished by first attaching the threaded PVC 'T' at the left of the photo to the broken piece on that side, while using a level (as previously described) to make sure the black sprinkler riser ends up perpendicular to ground level. Working on the other side of the break, where the large, notched piece is, we then attach to the right side of the break. The PVC patch is then manually telescoped out to the left, where it is secured to the threaded 'T' with PVC primer and then cement. You can see some PVC primer at the point of insertion.

IN CONCLUSION

I hope you've found this to be an enjoyable process. If you're anything like me, that sense of accomplishment you get as pull up to your house and see the results of your labor will add to this enjoyment.

The hard part is well behind you at this point. Any lawn requires maintenance – fertilizing, weed prevention or elimination, and occasionally at least partial potential replacement (though not a lot, and this should be handled with periodic over-seeding – preparing the soil and distributing more seed and seed cover over an already established lawn).

And, as I've noted above, no matter how careful you are, irrigation parts DO wear out from time to time, though not often. Sprinkler risers and sprinkler heads get damaged (most commonly by lawnmowers), valves can wear out, etc. Shifting into maintenance mode is actually pretty rewarding in itself – after all the work you've put in, you will probably be inclined to want to keep your lawn looking its best.

And besides, who doesn't want to have the nicest lawn in the neighborhood?

I certainly appreciate the time and trust you have shown in purchasing, reading and hopefully implementing the information contained in this E-book. I hope that you find (or perhaps even better yet, have found) the journey rewarding and would see fit to leave an honest review, which would be much appreciated..

Jon Lee

Made in the USA
Las Vegas, NV
10 July 2024